99 EASY-TO-USE
Speech and Language Activities

Instructions, patterns,
worksheets, and IEP objectives

by Cathy J. Williams, Kristine Vogt Sbaschnig,
Gloria H. Polk, Eileen A. Gleim

Illustrations by Pam Petersen

Duplicating

You may prefer to copy the designated reproducible materials by using stencils or spirit masters. It is not necessary to tear pages out of this book. Make a single photocopy of the desired page. Use that photocopy to make a stencil or spirit master on a thermal copier.

© 1984 by

Communication Skill Builders, Inc.
3130 N. Dodge Blvd./P.O. Box 42050
Tucson, Arizona 85733
(602) 323-7500

All rights reserved. Permission is granted for the user to photocopy and to make duplicating masters of those pages so indicated in limited form for instructional or administrative use only. No other parts of this book may be reproduced or transmitted in any form or by any means, electronic or mechanical, including photocopying and recording, or by any information storage and retrieval system, without written permission from the Publisher.

ISBN 0-88450-890-0   Catalog No. 7202

10 9 8 7 6 5 4 3 2 1
Printed in the United States of America

Acknowledgment

We wish to thank our families and all the teachers, students, and colleagues throughout the years who gave us ideas and inspired creativity.

About the Authors

These activities were developed during the authors' association at the Speech and Language Center of Wayne State University's Area of Communication Disorders and Science in Detroit.

Cathy J. Williams is a Clinical Supervisor and lecturer at Wayne State. Ms. Williams developed and supervises PLAY (Preschool Language Acquisition Years), a program for two- to five-year-olds. As the university coordinator for the public school practicum, she placed and supervised all student teachers in speech pathology. Previously she was a teacher of the speech and language impaired for the School District of the City of Pontiac. Ms. Williams is a graduate of Michigan State University, holding the M.A. degree in speech pathology and the B.A. with Honor in audiology and speech sciences.

Kristine Vogt Sbaschnig is a lecturer and Coordinator of Clinical Services, responsible for the daily administration of the Speech and Language Center. She supervises the clinical faculty and the graduate assistants, and determines the placement of all students for in-house-externship clinical practicum experiences. She has been employed as a speech-language pathologist in a variety of settings including the public schools, a sheltered workshop, and as chief of speech pathology services in an acute-care hospital. Ms. Sbaschnig received a B.A. and an M.A. degree in logopedics from Wichita State University.

Gloria H. Polk was a Clinical Supervisor and lecturer at the Speech and Language Center. She is now the Acting Director of speech pathology at Detroit Receiving Hospital and University Health Center. For a number of years she was manager of the Speech, Language, and Audiology Department, Wyandotte (Michigan) General Hospital. She has also been associated with Elkhart (Indiana) County Association for Retarded Children and has worked as a speech and language consultant in private practice. She holds the M.A. degree in speech and language pathology from Western Michigan University.

Eileen A. Gleim coauthored these materials while she was a Clinical Supervisor at the Speech and Language Center. During that time, she initiated and supervised a therapy program in English as a Second Language, as well as supervising the practicum hours of undergraduate and graduate students. She has been associated with the school districts of Schiller Park, Illinois, and Logansport, Indiana. Ms. Gleim is a graudate of Purdue University, holding the M.S. degree in speech pathology and B.S. with Highest Distinction in audiology and speech sciences.

Contents

POTPOURRI
- Whoo's in Speech? ... 3
- Speech and Language Calendar ... 6
- The Token Box ... 9
- Clem the Clown ... 10
- Four Games on a Gameboard ... 11
- Four Games on a Feltboard ... 12
- Passport through the Galaxy ... 13
- Rocket Ships ... 17

AUDITORY SKILLS
- Listening Boxes ... 21
- My Listening Book ... 22
- Hidden Phonemes ... 26

ARTICULATION SKILLS
- Bullseye ... 31
- Definitions ... 33
- Calico Cat ... 36
- Oral-Motor Ferris Wheel ... 37
- Three Sound Placement Activities ... 40
- The Rabbit and the Turtle ... 47
- Speech Therapy Finger Play ... 49
- Sound Pockets ... 51
- Four Gameboards for Practicing Sounds in Syllables ... 53
- Hide and Say Games ... 59
- Sound Mazes ... 60
- Speech Puzzles ... 63
- Two or More ... 64
- Word Bingo ... 66

LANGUAGE SKILLS
- Shapes and Colors ... 71
- Classification Folders ... 72
- Holiday Matching ... 73
- Concept File Folder ... 74
- Sentence Spin ... 75
- Fishbowl ... 76
- Clue Box ... 79
- Language Stimulation Using the Sense of Touch ... 80
- People-Sorting ... 82
- Plurals File Folder ... 83
- The WH? House ... 84
- The WH? Spinner ... 85
- Question Games ... 87
- Treasure Hunt Maze ... 88
- Coaster Card Game ... 89

COMBINATION SKILLS

- Seven Easy Puppets 93
- Battlefield 102
- Roll the Cubes 103
- Grocery Store 104
- View-It 105
- The Speech Can 106
- Match the Shapes 107
- Find the Squirrel 109
- Articulation/Language Spinner 111
- Magic Number Board 112
- Target Word Board 113
- Circle Drill 114
- Toy Town 115
- TV Talk 116
- Concentration 117
- Newspaper Activities 118
- Role-Playing Activities 119
- Santa's Speech 125

Potpourri

Whoo's in Speech?

This is an appropriate activity for the first day of speech-language class.

Suggested grade levels: Kindergarten - 6

Objective: To identify and unify the students in speech and language classes

Materials
- Black construction paper
- Orange construction paper
- Orange tagboard
- Marking pens
- Glue

Preparation
Using black construction paper, cut out an owl shape (Pattern 1) for each student. Cut out an owl face (Pattern 2) for each owl, using orange construction paper. On orange tagboard, make a sign: WHOO'S IN SPEECH?

Procedure
Give each student an owl shape and an owl face. Have them glue the face on their owls and write their name by its beak. The students place their completed owls around the WHOO'S IN SPEECH? sign. Emphasize that these are all the students in the speech-language class and how special they are. (Be sure to make an owl for yourself!)

PATTERN 1

Whoo's in Speech?
(Owl Shape)

© 1984 by Communication Skill Builders, Inc.
This page may be reproduced for instructional use.

PATTERN 2

Whoo's in Speech?
(Owl Face)

©1984 by Communication Skill Builders, Inc.
This page may be reproduced for instructional use.

Speech and Language Calendar

A master Speech and Language Calendar hung in the speech classroom provides excellent opening and closing activities.

Suggested grade levels: Kindergarten - 6

Objectives: 1. To develop carryover of speech and language skills
2. To develop time concepts

Materials
Calendars
Crayons

Preparation
Reproduce calendars, using Pattern 3. Write a speech or language task in each square, using the calendar tasks listed below.

Procedure
At the beginning of every month, give each student a calendar. Discuss the season and the events and holidays that will occur during the month. Ask each student to decorate the border of the calendar with pictures that illustrate the time of year. Send the calendar home with the student. Request that the calendar be displayed on the refrigerator or on a home bulletin board. The student does the speech activity each day and marks an X on the calendar when the task is completed. The student returns the calendar at the end of the month and the clinician reviews the tasks.

CALENDAR TASKS

1. Name a holiday that has your sound.
2. Say a sentence using the past tense.
3. Name an animal that has your sound.
4. Write a number that has your sound. Say it three times.
5. Use the verbs *is* and *are* in a sentence.
6. Use two words that have your sound at the end in a sentence.
7. Name something you ate yesterday. Make up a sentence about it.
8. Name something from the circus that has your sound.
9. Tell about a TV show you watched.
10. Name a month that has your sound.
11. Draw a picture of something that has your sound.
12. Tell your mother a story about your picture.
13. Name something from the grocery that has your sound.
14. Name three words that have your sound in the middle.
15. Tell me a fruit or vegetable that has your sound.

16. Name something from your room that has your sound.
17. Name a toy that has your sound.
18. Name the days of the week.
19. Tell your mother three things you did yesterday.
20. Count from one to twenty.
21. Read a page from your favorite book.
22. Listen for your sound on the radio. Say the word three times.
23. Tell your father three words that have your sound at the end.
24. Name a rock group or song that has your sound.
25. Name a shape that has your sound.
26. Tell Mom why these words are alike: lock/key.
27. Tell Dad how these words are alike: mouse/house.
28. Tell Mom two things you'll do tomorrow.
29. Say a boy's or girl's name that has your sound.
30. Name something from school that has your sound.
31. Name a city or state that has your sound.

PATTERN 3

Speech and Language Calendar

© 1984 by Communication Skill Builders, Inc.
This page may be reproduced for instructional use.

The Token Box

Students can visually measure their progress with this valuable tool.

Suggested grade levels: Preschool - 2

Objective: Token reinforcement

Materials
    An egg carton for each student

    Pennies, chips, or circles cut out of construction paper

Preparation
    Cut off the top of each egg carton.

Procedure
    A token is placed in a section of the egg carton for a correct response.

Clem the Clown

Suggested grade levels: Preschool - 2

Objective: Token reinforcement

Materials
- 2 cardboard ice-cream buckets
- Scissors
- Marking pens
- Tape
- Construction paper

Preparation
In one bucket, cut three holes to resemble eyes and a mouth. Use marking pens to decorate the face to look like a clown. Decorate the other bucket to resemble a clown's hat. Tape it to the top of the "face." Cut construction paper into 1-inch circles representing balls.

Procedure
After a correct response, the student "feeds" the clown a ball.

Four Games on a Gameboard

Suggested grade levels: Preschool - 6

Objectives: Any objective that can be accomplished by use of stimulus cards

Materials
  Tagboard
  Stimulus cards

Preparation
  Cut tagboard into 9-inch by 12-inch rectangles. Draw Tic-Tac-Toe lines to make nine squares on each board. Make one board for each student in the group. Place one or more stimulus cards on each square.

Procedures
  1. Play Tic-Tac-Toe. Two students share one board, playing Tic-Tac-Toe as they respond with each stimulus card.
  2. Play Find the Surprise. Each student receives a board. The clinician hides a small star, a paper clip, or other small token on one square of each board, under the stimulus cards. The students take turns choosing squares on their boards and responding with the cards on that square. Any student who finds the hidden token gets one point.
  3. Play Lotto. Each student receives a board, with a stimulus card on each square. In turn, each student receives a stimulus card which is matched to a card already on the board.
  4. Play Bingo. Each column and each row on the board is labeled, and a stimulus card is placed on each square. As the clinician calls out the code for a square, the students respond with the stimulus card on that board, then turn the card face down. Play continues until someone gets "Bingo."

Four Games on a Feltboard

Suggested grade levels: Kindergarten - 3

Objectives: Any objective that can be accomplished through the use of stimulus materials

Materials
- 18-inch by 24-inch piece of heavy cardboard
- 22-inch by 28-inch piece of solid colored felt
- Squares of felt or scraps of flannel
- Stapler
- Scissors

Preparation
Lay the felt flat and put the cardboard on top of it. Fold over 2 inches of excess felt on one side at a time, and staple it to the cardboard. Fold in the corners and staple them down. This is the back of the feltboard.

Cut out simple objects, foods, shapes, animals, etc., from the felt squares or flannel scraps.

Procedures
1. *Sorting and Classifying*
   Have a pile of cutouts ready. Ask the student to put all like objects on the board (for example, all yellow objects, or all foods, etc.).

2. *Identifying Objects*
   Have the student find a specific cutout and put it on the board; or you can put an object on the board for identification or description.

3. *Following Directions and Spatial Relationships*
   Give the student one- to four-level commands to follow.

4. *Expressive Language and Sequencing*
   Give the student cutouts that create a story. Ask the student to retell the story.

Passport through the Galaxy

Suggested grade levels: Kindergarten - 3

Objective: To develop incentive for speech/language progress

Materials
  Copies of pages 14-16
  Stapler
  Stickers

Preparation
  Reproduce the following three pages. Staple them together to make a booklet.

Procedure
  Discuss appropriate speech/language goals with the student. Label each square on the "Planet Permits" page with a planet name (representing the desired goal). Upon achieving the goal, the student puts a sticker in the square for having "traveled" to that planet.

PASSPORT THROUGH THE GALAXY

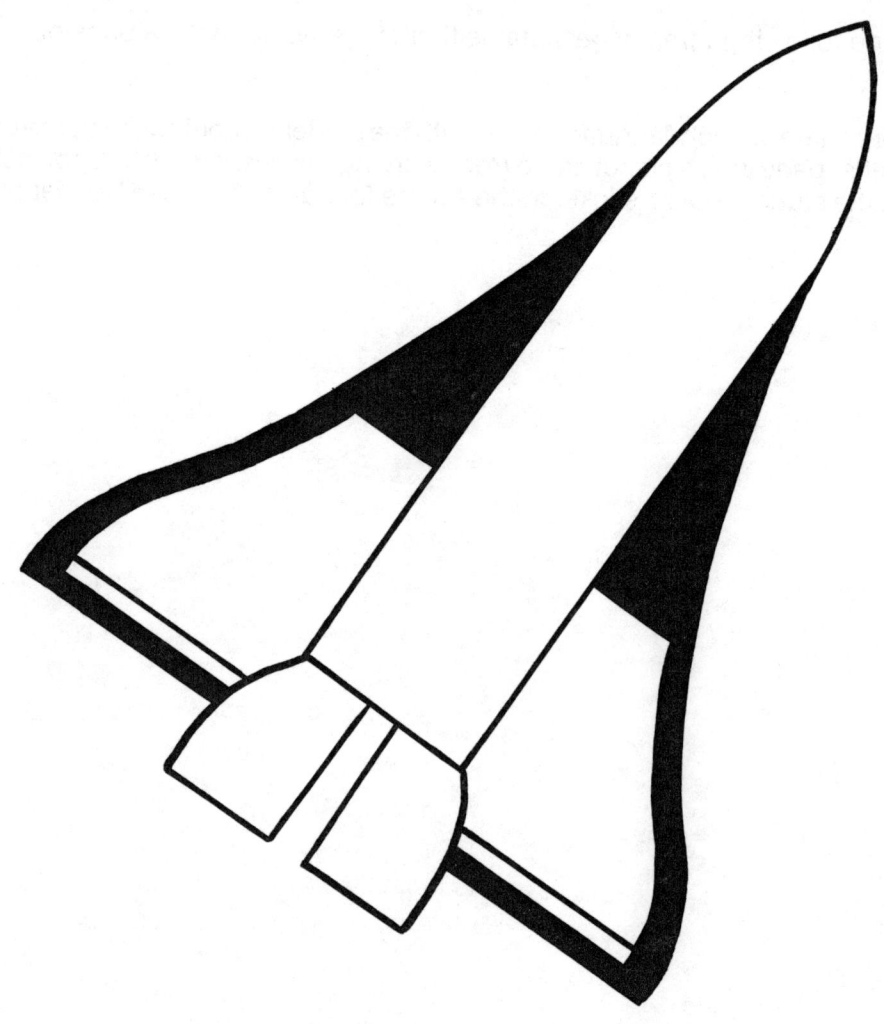

Passport through the Galaxy

Identification

Creature's Name:	
Date of Birth:	
Home Planet:	
Language Spoken:	
Reason for Passport:	
Issue Date:	Expiration Date:

Paste photo here

Passport through the Galaxy

Planet Permits

Planet:	Planet:
Planet:	Planet:
Planet:	Planet:
Planet:	Planet:
Planet:	Planet:

Rocket Ships

This is a combination opening-closing activity.

Suggested grade levels: Kindergarten - 6

Objectives: To promote carryover of speech and language skills

Materials
    Construction paper
    Scissors
    Paper punch
    Metal shower hooks
    Containers
    Stimulus pictures
    Glue

Preparation
    For each student, make ten rocket ships from construction paper, using Pattern 4. Punch a hole in the top of each rocket, and place ten rockets on each shower hook. Label the containers with target phonemes and language concepts. Sort the stimulus pictures into the containers.

Procedure
    At the beginning of each session, the student selects a stimulus picture appropriate to the therapy objectives, and glues it on one of the rockets. During the session, the student works on the target phoneme or language concept. At the close of each session, the student produces the target phoneme or language concept.

    When the student finishes the rockets (ten pictures) send them home to promote carryover of speech and language skills.

PATTERN 4
Rocket Ships

©1984 by Communication Skill Builders, Inc.
This page may be reproduced for instructional use.

Auditory Skills

Listening Boxes

Suggested grade levels: Kindergarten - 4

Objective: To develop auditory discrimination skills

Materials
- Tagboard
- Scissors
- Marking pen
- Empty frozen juice cans
- Paint or colorful adhesive plastic
- Masking tape
- Materials that make sounds when shaken (pennies, small balls, rice, salt, bells, water, etc.)

Preparation
Cut tagboard into rectangular "answer boards," and draw outlines for placing two containers on each board. Paint the juice cans, or cover them with adhesive plastic. Make "sound pairs" by placing materials in sets of two containers. Seal the containers with tape.

Procedure
The student sorts the containers by the sounds they make, placing each "sound pair" together on an answer board.

Optional
You may wish to use baby-food or other small glass jars. At the end of the activity, the student may remove the lids to see the materials that make various sounds.

My Listening Book

This activity is particularly beneficial at the beginning of the school year to develop and strengthen auditory skills.

Suggested grade levels: Kindergarten - 6

Objectives: 1. To develop auditory discrimination skills
2. To develop categorization skills

Materials
Tagboard
Copies of Worksheet 1 (10 for each student)
Environmental sounds tape
Brass fasteners
Magazines, scissors, paste

Preparation
Using tagboard, make two listening ears (Patterns 5 and 6) for book covers. Add ten pages of Worksheet 1, and fasten with brass fasteners to make a booklet.

Procedure
The clinician plays a tape recording of sounds (around the house, farm, city, zoo, school; outdoor sounds, noisy sounds, quiet sounds). The students are asked to identify each sound.

After the students have heard the tape, they are instructed to find magazine pictures of ten items that can be heard in that environment, cut them out, and paste them in the Listening Book.

The clinician asks the student, "What do you like to hear?" The student responds with the carrier sentence, "My ears like to hear _____."

PATTERN 5

My Listening Book (Front Cover)

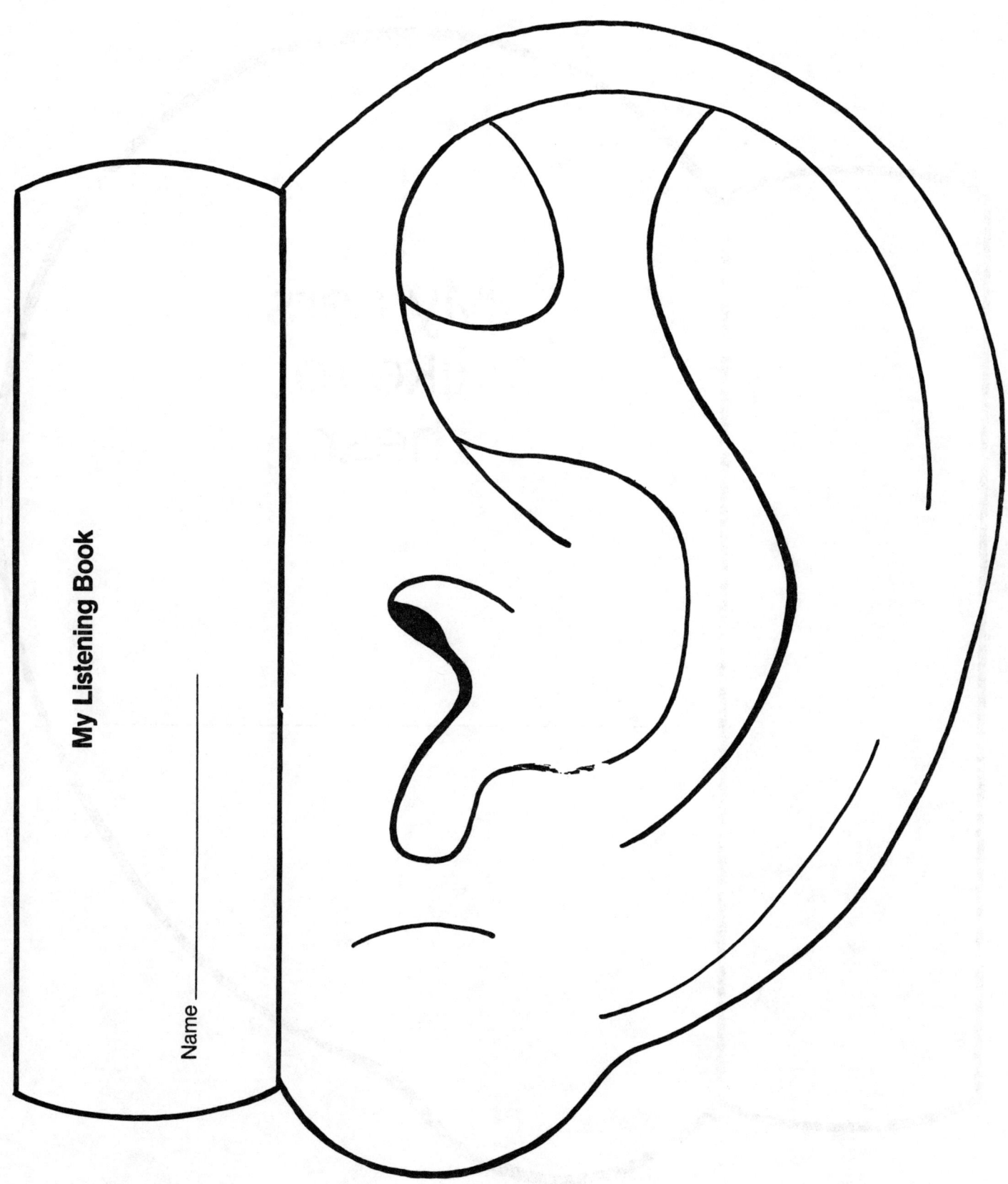

©1984 by Communication Skill Builders, Inc.
This page may be reproduced for instructional use.

WORKSHEET 1

My Listening Book (Pages)

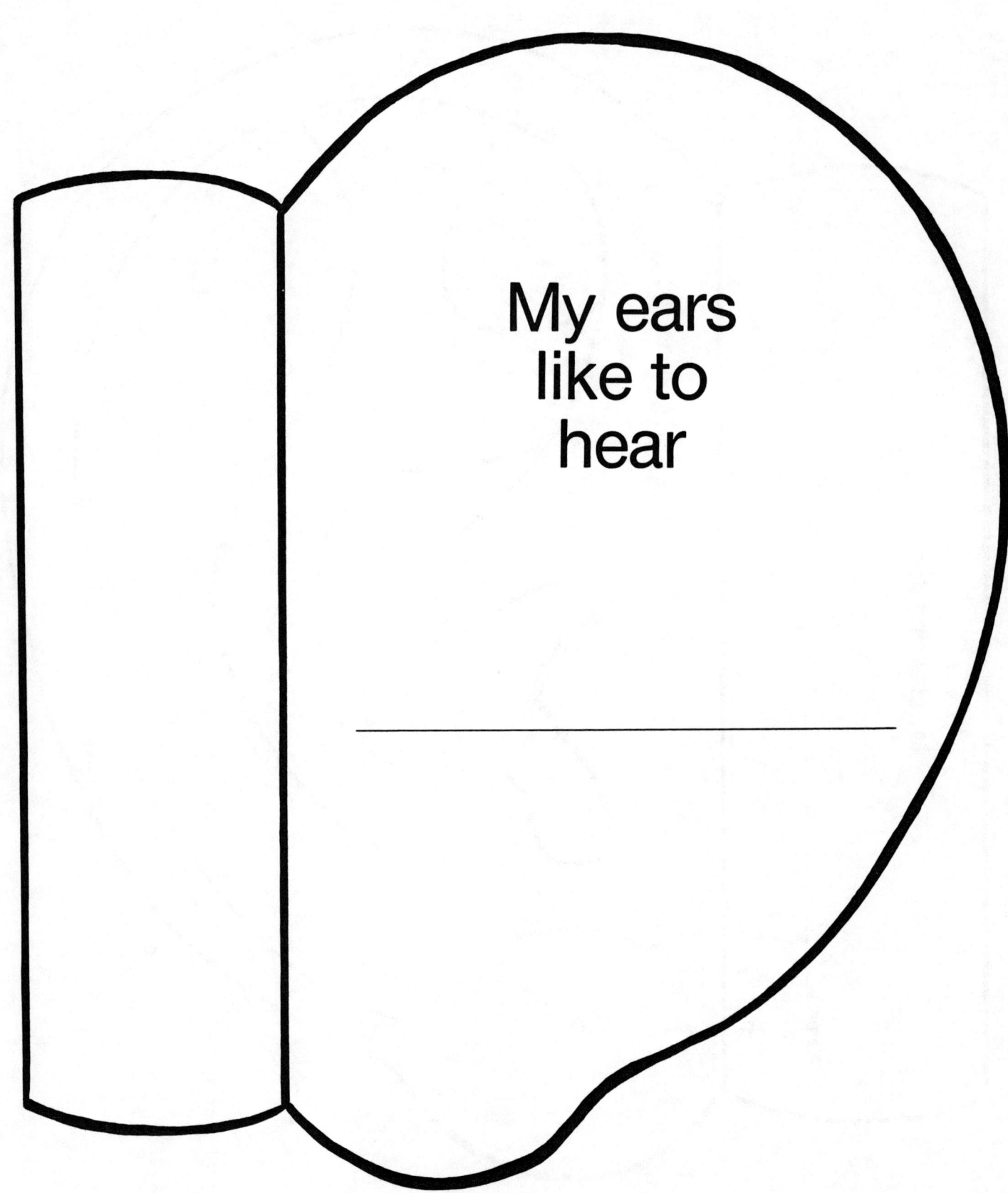

My ears like to hear

_____

PATTERN 6
My Listening Book (Back Cover)

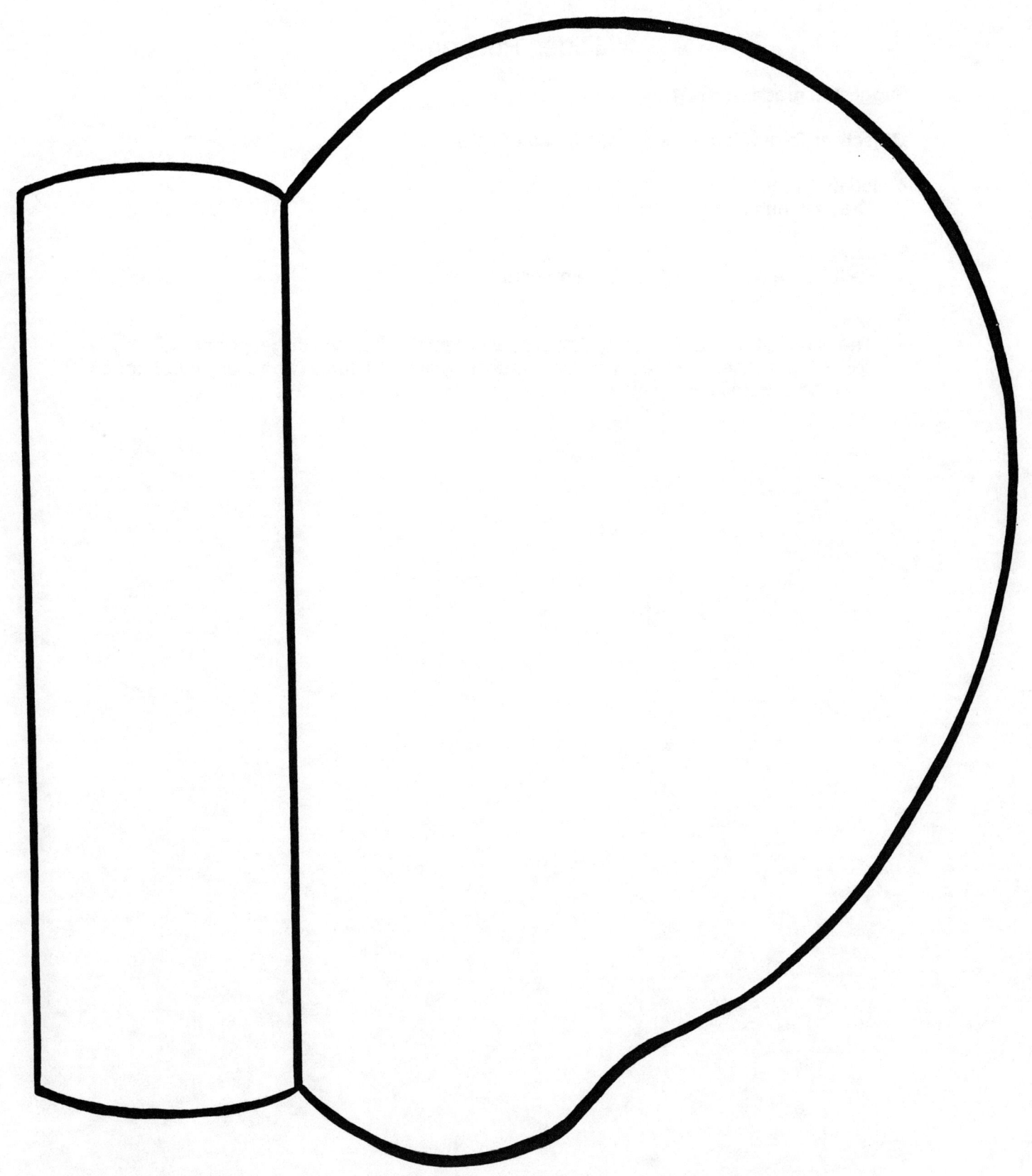

Hidden Phonemes

Suggested grade levels: 1 - 4

Objective: To develop auditory discrimination skills

Materials
Crayons numbered 1, 2, 3, 4

Preparation
Reproduce Worksheet 2 for each student.

Procedure
The clinician says a phoneme. The student identifies it as the target phoneme. After a correct response, the student colors one section of the picture. The activity is continued until the picture is completed.

WORKSHEET 2
Hidden Phonemes

©1984 by Communication Skill Builders, Inc.
This page may be reproduced for instructional use.

Articulation Skills

Bullseye

This is an excellent activity when drilling a new phoneme.

Suggested grade levels: Kindergarten - 6

Objective: To develop articulation skills

Materials
    Tagboard
    Construction paper
    Scissors
    Stimulus cards

Preparation
    Construct a target out of tagboard, using Pattern 7. Cut out several arrows from construction paper.

Procedure
    Write the target phoneme in the center of the target. The student produces the phoneme in isolation or at the word, phrase, or sentence level. A correct production scores a bullseye and an arrow is placed in the center of the target. If the production is approximated, the arrow is placed on the target. If the production is incorrect, the arrow is placed below the target.

PATTERN 7
Bullseye

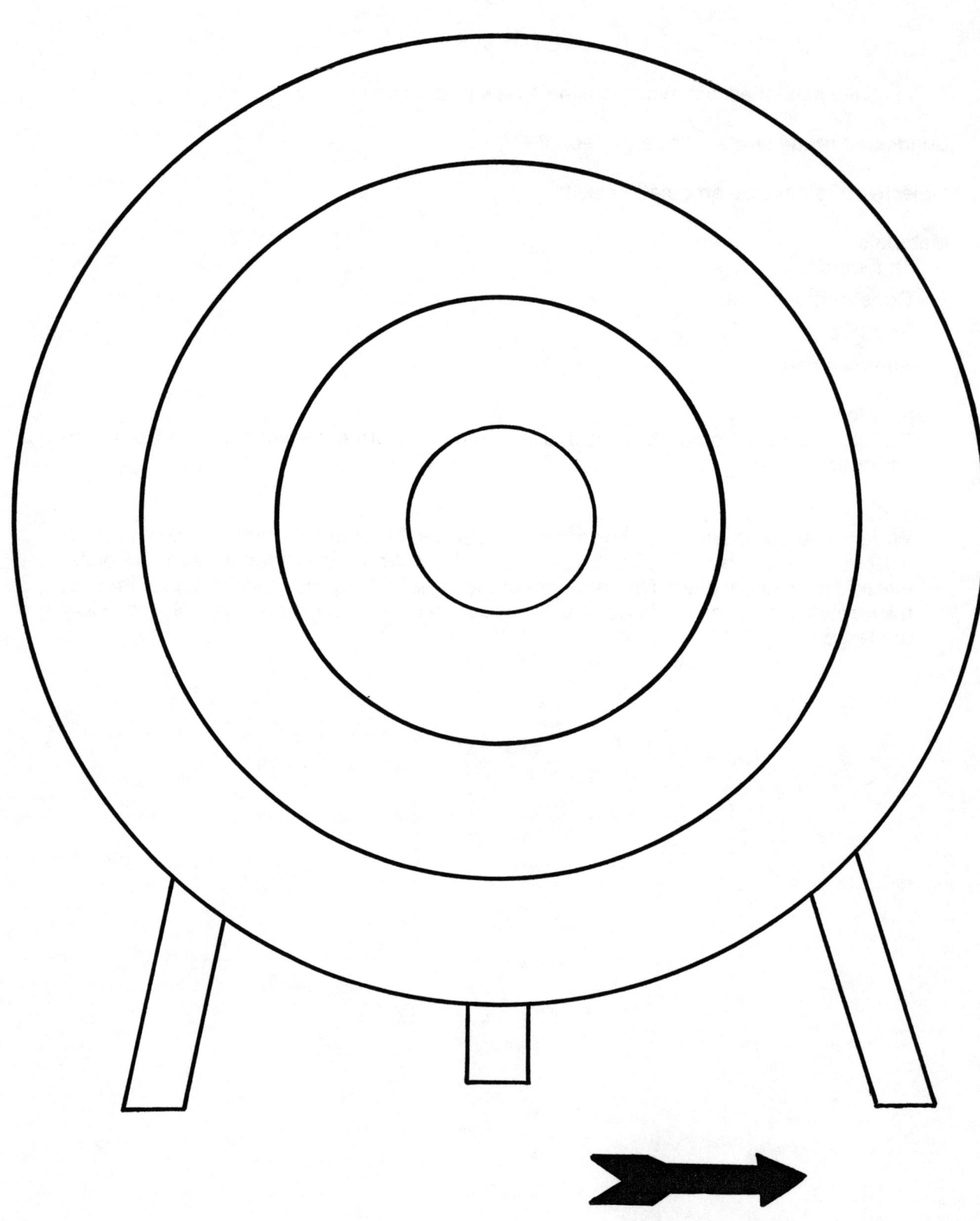

©1984 by Communication Skill Builders, Inc.
This page may be reproduced for instructional use.

Definitions

This is an excellent opening or closing drill.

Suggested grade levels: 2 - 6

Objective: To develop correct production of the target phonemes /s/, /r/, and /l/

Materials
   Drill 1, 2, or 3

Preparation
   None

Procedure
   The clinician reads a definition to the student. The student responds with the appropriate word and uses it in a sentence.

DRILL 1
/s/ Definitions

1. The evening meal (supper)
2. Not feeling well (sick)
3. The ocean (sea)
4. Two numbers that follow five (six, seven)
5. A girl's name
6. Something to wash with (soap)
7. Popeye's favorite food (spinach)
8. You use it with pepper (salt)
9. Lettuce, tomatoes, and dressing (salad)
10. One penny (cent)
11. Not sweet (sour)
12. First day of the week (Sunday)
13. The opposite of last (first)
14. What we write with (pencil)
15. Not very neat (messy)
16. You and me (us)
17. The opposite of more (less)
18. A four-legged animal you can ride (horse)
19. A building you live in (house)
20. Green stuff that covers the ground (grass)
21. December holiday (Christmas)
22. Cowboy's rope (lasso)
23. Frozen water (ice)
24. What you might eat for lunch (sandwich, soup, etc.)
25. Where your mother keeps her money (purse)

DRILL 2
/r/ Definitions

1. Faster than walking — (running)
2. Water falling from the sky — (rain)
3. Jewelry for fingers — (ring)
4. Animal with long ears and fluffy tail — (rabbit)
5. The shape of a circle — (round)
6. A color that makes bulls mad — (red)
7. Correct — (right)
8. Top of a house — (roof)
9. What you learn to do in first grade — (read)
10. This animal wakes you up on the farm — (rooster)
11. To steal — (rob)
12. A color, also a juice you drink for breakfast — (orange)
13. Mistake — (wrong)
14. Animal with a long, long neck — (giraffe)
15. Noise that a happy cat makes — (purr)
16. Tool used to pound nails — (hammer)
17. Noise an angry lion makes — (roar)
18. Number after three — (four)
19. What you shoot from a bow — (arrow)
20. An animal with antlers — (deer)
21. Your parents — (mother, father)
22. What you look in to see yourself — (mirror)
23. What you mail — (letter)
24. What you drive — (car)
25. A vegetable that rabbits eat — (carrot)

DRILL 3
/l/ Definitions

1. What fire fighters climb — (ladder)
2. The opposite of big — (little)
3. The mailman brings this — (letter, mail)
4. An animal that roars — (lion)
5. What you do when you're happy — (laugh, smile)
6. You need a key to open this — (lock)
7. A sour, yellow fruit — (lemon)
8. Part of a tree — (leaf)
9. Another word for sucker — (lollipop)
10. A famous president — (Lincoln)
11. What you use your ears for — (listening)
12. At night you lay your head on this — (pillow)
13. A person who arrests criminals — (police officer)
14. A person who flies an airplane — (pilot)
15. The color of sunshine — (yellow)
16. What you blow out on your birthday — (candle)
17. The meal in the middle of the day — (lunch)
18. What we sit at when we eat — (table)
19. We hit this with a bat — (ball)
20. The opposite of push — (pull)
21. A three-sided shape — (triangle)
22. A red fruit that grows in a tree — (apple)
23. Football players do this — (tackle, huddle)
24. You dry with this — (towel)
25. This has pieces you put together — (puzzle)

Calico Cat

Suggested grade levels: Kindergarten - 3

Objective: To stimulate oral motor musculature

Material
A mirror

Preparation
Fold along the dotted line, below; reproduce Worksheet 3 for each student.

Procedure
The clinician and the student face the mirror. (The clinician should be at the student's eye level.) The clinician demonstrates each oral motor exercise. Then the student performs the exercise.

WORKSHEET 3

Calico Cat has just finished a saucer of milk and is ready to wash its face. Pretend you are a cat, and wash your face, too.

1. Stretch your tongue to lick a drop of milk off your nose.

2. Stretch your tongue to lick the milk from your chin.

3. Stretch your tongue to each corner of your mouth to lick the milk from your whiskers.

4. Lick your top lip and your bottom lip.

5. Lick your lips around and around, first in one direction and then in the other.

6. Stretch your tongue and lick every tooth clean.

7. Hold your tongue to the roof of your mouth. Count to five. Now, lick the roof of your mouth all the way to your throat.

© 1984 by Communication Skill Builders, Inc.
This page may be reproduced for instructional use.

Oral-Motor Ferris Wheel

Suggested grade levels: Kindergarten - 6

Objective: To develop proper placement of target phonemes

Materials
  Construction paper
  Tagboard
  Scissors
  Glue
  Marking pen
  Stimulus pictures

Preparation
  Using construction paper, cut out twelve flaps (Pattern 8) and one circle (Pattern 9). From tagboard, cut six strips, each 1 inch by 9 inches. Glue each strip to the center of the circle. Glue two flaps on each strip to make the Ferris wheel. On the center circle, write the target phoneme. Glue a stimulus picture on the outside of each flap. Inside the flap, draw the speech helper symbols (Pattern 10).

Procedure
  The student produces the target word, and tells the clinician which speech helpers were used. The student then lifts the flap to self-check the answer.

PATTERN 8

Flap for Oral-Motor Ferris Wheel

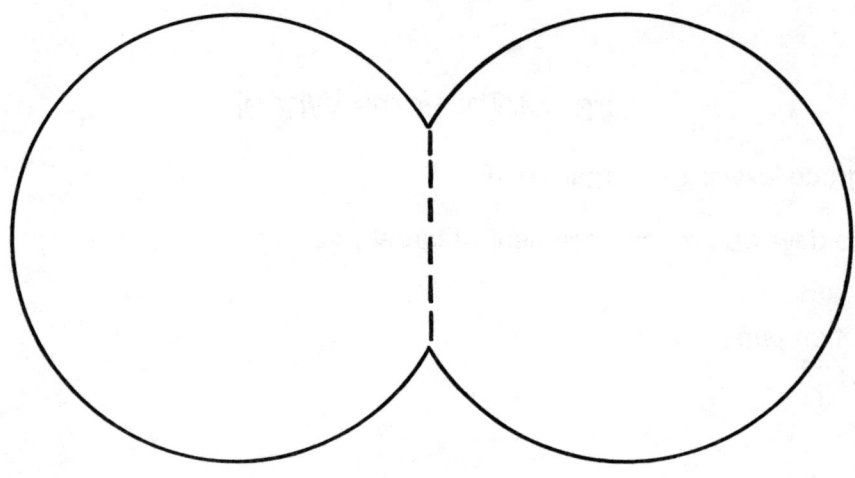

PATTERN 9

Center Circle for Oral-Motor Ferris Wheel

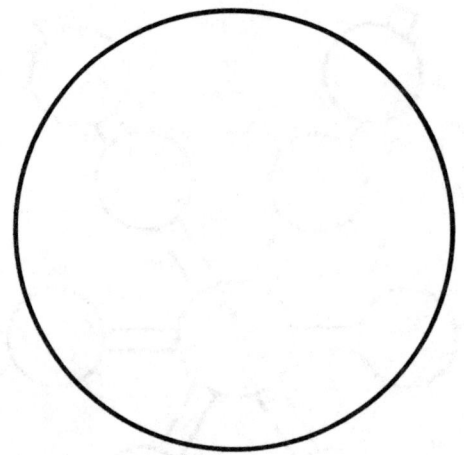

©1984 by Communication Skill Builders, Inc.
This page may be reproduced for instructional use.

PATTERN 10

Symbols for Speech Helpers

lips

teeth

voice box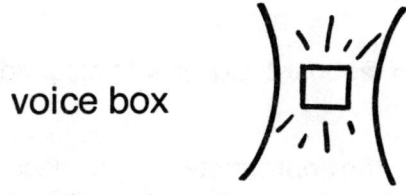

tongue)

Three Sound Placement Activities

Suggested grade levels: Kindergarten - 6

Objectives:
1. To develop proper placement for phonemes
2. To develop the production of the phonemes /e, i, o, u, a/, /p, b, m, t, d, t, f, θ/
3. To develop oral-motor sequencing for phonemes

1. "GEORGE"

Materials
Tagboard
Clear adhesive plastic
Crayon
Tissue or soft cloth

Preparation
Reproduce Patterns 11-A and 11B on tagboard. Cover with clear adhesive plastic.

Procedure
The clinician uses the crayon to draw the appropriate tongue placement for the target phoneme. The student imitates the tongue placement and produces the sound. The clinician wipes the board and draws another tongue placement.

Optional
The clinician may wish to make a set of permanent tongue placement pictures. Reproduce the patterns a number of times, draw a tongue placement picture on each, then cover with plastic.

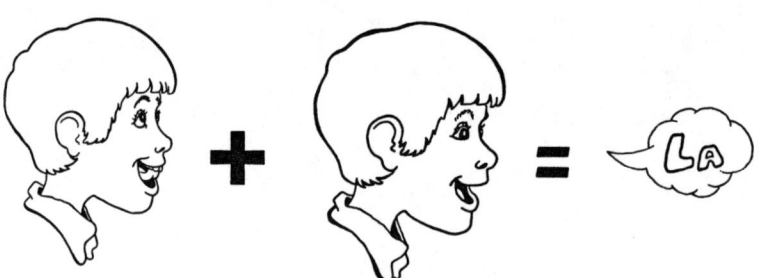

2. "LIPPY"

Materials
- Tagboard
- Pieces of corrugated cardboard, each 5½ inches wide by 4½ inches high
- Scissors
- Small magnets
- Tape
- Construction paper
- Marking pens
- Paper clips
- Glue

Preparation

On each cardboard piece, about an inch from the bottom, cut out a section (the same size as the magnet) from the first corrugated layer. *(Do not* cut all the way through the cardboard.) Place the magnet in the cut-out section and secure it with tape. Reproduce "Lippy" (Pattern 12) on construction paper and glue it over the cardboard. Reproduce lips (Pattern 12), cut them out, and glue a paper clip on the back of each.

Procedure

The clinician places the desired lip position on "Lippy." The student is asked to produce the sound that "Lippy" is making.

This activity can be done imitatively or spontaneously and can be expanded to words. A combination of lip positions can be used for sequencing sounds.

Magnet covered with construction paper

Back of lip pattern, showing paper clip glued on

3. ORAL-MOTOR EXERCISES

Materials
- Worksheet 4
- Recordkeeping Form
- "George" and/or "Lippy" models
- A mirror

Preparation

Reproduce Worksheet 4 and Recordkeeping Form (page 46).

Procedure

The clinician and the student face the mirror. (The clinician should be at the student's eye level.) The clinician has the student perform the exercises on Worksheet 4, using "George" or "Lippy" as stimulus. The student performs each exercise imitatively, then spontaneously. The student's performance is charted daily on the recordkeeping form.

PATTERN 11-A
"George"

PATTERN 11-B
"George"

PATTERN 12

"Lippy"

X

Consonants m, p, b

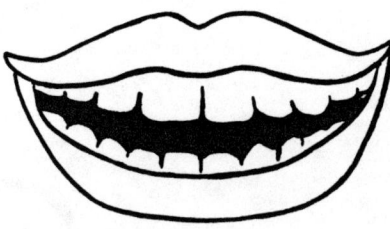

Vowel e

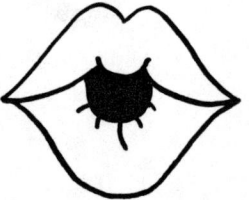

Vowel o

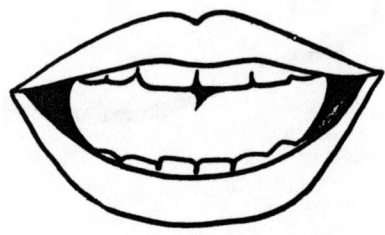

Vowels a, i

©1984 by Communication Skill Builders, Inc.
This page may be reproduced for instructional use.

WORKSHEET 4
Oral-Motor Exercises

These exercises are a hierarchy of oral-motor movements without sound imitatively and spontaneously, and then oral-motor movements with sound imitatively and spontaneously.

Level 1. Do these phonemes, without sound imitatively:
- a. /o/
- b. /e/
- c. /i/
- d. /u/
- e. /ae/
- f. /p/—lips together, not pursed, bilabial position
- g. /l/—tongue behind front teeth, tongue tip position
- h. /th/—tongue between teeth

Level 2. Repeat the above phonemes, without sound spontaneously. For spontaneous productions, use "Lippy" or "George" for visual stimulation.

Level 3. Repeat the phonemes in Level 1, with sound imitatively.

Level 4. Repeat the phonemes in Level 1, with sound spontaneously.

In Levels 5 and 6, the phonemes are to be blended to form a nonsense syllable.

Level 5.
- a. Blend two vowels (such as /i/ /o/), without sound imitatively.
- b. Repeat the above, without sound spontaneously.
- c. Blend a vowel and a consonant (such as /o/ /f/) or a consonant and a vowel (such as /p/ /e/), without sound imitatively.
- d. Repeat the above, without sound spontaneously.
- e. Blend three vowels (such as /e/ /i/ /o/), without sound imitatively.
- f. Repeat the above, without sound spontaneously.
- g. Blend three phonemes using consonants and vowels (such as /l/ /o/ /p/), without sound imitatively.
- h. Repeat the above, without sound spontaneously.

Level 6. Repeat the steps in Level 5, using sound.

ORAL-MOTOR EXERCISES

Recordkeeping Form

Name: _____   Date: _____

Age: _____   Diagnosis: _____

Level 1 Steps

Trials	a.	b.	c.	d.	e.	f.	g.	h.
1								
2								
3								
4								
5								
6								
7								
8								
9								
10								
% Correct								

Level 2 Steps

Trials	a.	b.	c.	d.	e.	f.	g.	h.
1								
2								
3								
4								
5								
6								
7								
8								
9								
10								
% Correct								

Level 3 Steps

Trials	a.	b.	c.	d.	e.	f.	g.	h.
1								
2								
3								
4								
5								
6								
7								
8								
9								
10								
% Correct								

Level 4 Steps

Trials	a.	b.	c.	d.	e.	f.	g.	h.
1								
2								
3								
4								
5								
6								
7								
8								
9								
10								
% Correct								

Level 5 Steps

Trials	a.	b.	c.	d.	e.	f.	g.	h.
1								
2								
3								
4								
5								
6								
7								
8								
9								
10								
% Correct								

Level 6 Steps

Trials	a.	b.	c.	d.	e.	f.	g.	h.
1								
2								
3								
4								
5								
6								
7								
8								
9								
10								
% Correct								

© 1984 by Communication Skill Builders, Inc.
This form may be reproduced for administrative use.

The Rabbit and the Turtle

Suggested grade levels: 2 - 6

Objective: To develop a normal speaking rate

Materials:
    Two wooden ice-cream sticks
    Tagboard
    Glue or stapler

Preparation
    Make a rabbit and a turtle from tagboard (Pattern 13). Attach each to a wooden ice-cream stick.

Procedure
    Explain to the student that a turtle walks very slowly and a rabbit runs very fast.

    Tell a story and ask the student to hold up the rabbit when your rate is too rapid. Then ask the student to converse, and you hold up the turtle to signal that the student's rate of speech is appropriate.

PATTERN 13

The Rabbit and the Turtle

©1984 by Communication Skill Builders, Inc.
This page may be reproduced for instructional use.

Speech Therapy Finger Play

Suggested grade levels: Preschool - 2

Objective: To develop production of the target phoneme in syllables

Materials
   Construction paper
   Tape
   Copies of Worksheet 5

Preparation
   Reproduce, cut out, and tape the finger puppets (Pattern 14).
   Fold along the dotted line; reproduce Worksheet 5 for each student.

Procedure
   The student places a finger puppet on each finger, and recites the finger play "Five Little People," using the target phoneme.
   Finger puppets may also be used to develop interactive language skills.

WORKSHEET 5
Five Little People

Five little people, smiling all day,
Waiting for speech class. What did they say?
One said "Say!"
One said "See!"
One said "Sigh!"
One said "So!"
One said "Soo-oo-oo!"

PATTERN 14

Finger Puppets

Cut out and tape the strip to fit each finger.

©1984 by Communication Skill Builders, Inc.
This page may be reproduced for instructional use.

Sound Pockets

Suggested grade level: Kindergarten - 2

Objectives: 1. To develop articulation skills
2. To develop auditory discrimination skills

Materials
Fabric scraps
Buttons, lace, and other trim
Ribbon
Stimulus cards

Preparation
Using Pattern 15, make a pocket for the clinician and one for each student in the group. Decorate the pockets with rickrack, ruffles, or letters representing the target phoneme. Attach ribbon so that the pockets may be tied around the waist. Place stimulus cards in the clinician's pocket.

Procedures
1. Each student selects a stimulus card from the clinician's pocket and produces the target phoneme in a word, phrase, or sentence. If the response is correct, the stimulus card is placed in the student's pocket.
2. The student selects a stimulus card from the clinician's pocket and determines whether the word contains the target phoneme. If it does, the stimulus card is placed in the student's pocket.

Clinical Note
For production of /ʃ/, draw the outline of a shirt on tagboard and staple or glue a pocket to the shirt.

PATTERN 15

Sound Pockets

Cut out two pieces and sew them together to make each pocket.

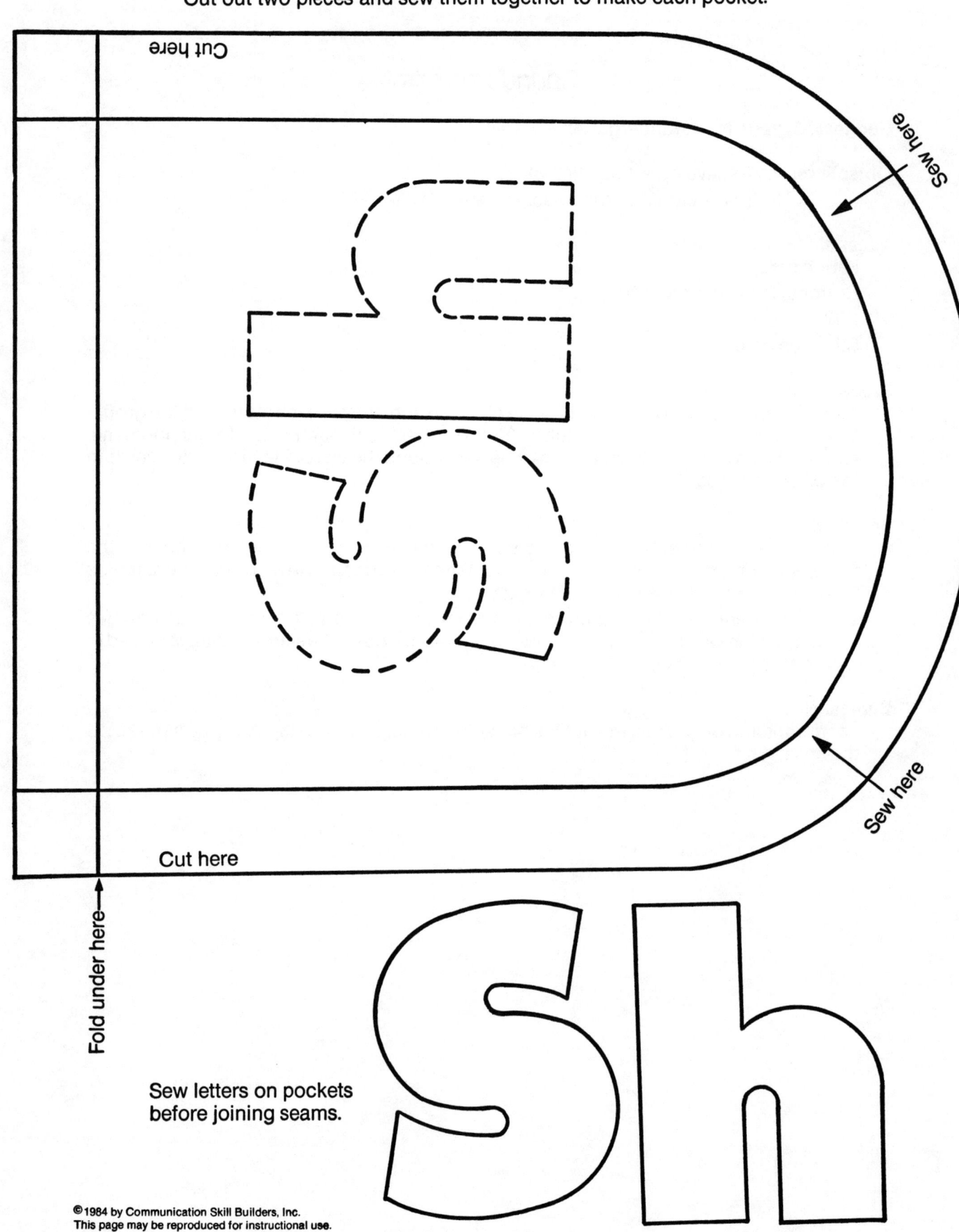

Sew letters on pockets before joining seams.

©1984 by Communication Skill Builders, Inc.
This page may be reproduced for instructional use.

Four Gameboards for Practicing Sounds in Syllables

Suggested grade levels: Preschool - 6

Objective: To develop production of the target phoneme in syllables

1. THE SOUND STAIRS

Materials
Tagboard
Clear adhesive plastic

Preparation
Reproduce Pattern 16 on tagboard. Cover with clear adhesive plastic.

Procedure
Ask the student to produce the syllable slowly while "climbing up each stair" and quickly while "climbing down each stair."

2. THE SOUND STREET

Materials
Tagboard
Clear adhesive plastic
A small toy car

Preparation
Reproduce Pattern 17 on tagboard. Cover with clear adhesive plastic.

Procedure
The long (vertical) street is named the target phoneme (for example, "S" Street). The student prolongs the target phoneme while "driving the car down the street" and adds the vowel sound when "turning onto a side street."

3. THE SOUND PARACHUTE

Materials
- Tagboard
- A crayon
- Clear adhesive plastic
- Tissue or soft cloth

Preparation
Reproduce Pattern 18 on tagboard. Cover with clear adhesive plastic. Use the crayon to write the target phoneme on the parachute. (Later, wipe it off with a tissue and reuse the worksheet.)

Procedure
The student produces the target phoneme, then adds the vowel sound while pointing to the vowel on each string.

4. THE SOUND SLIDE

Materials
- Tagboard
- Clear adhesive plastic

Preparation
Reproduce Pattern 19 on tagboard. Cover with clear adhesive plastic.

Procedure
The student practices the target phoneme while "climbing the steps on the slide," then adds a vowel while "sliding down."

PATTERN 16

The Sound Stairs

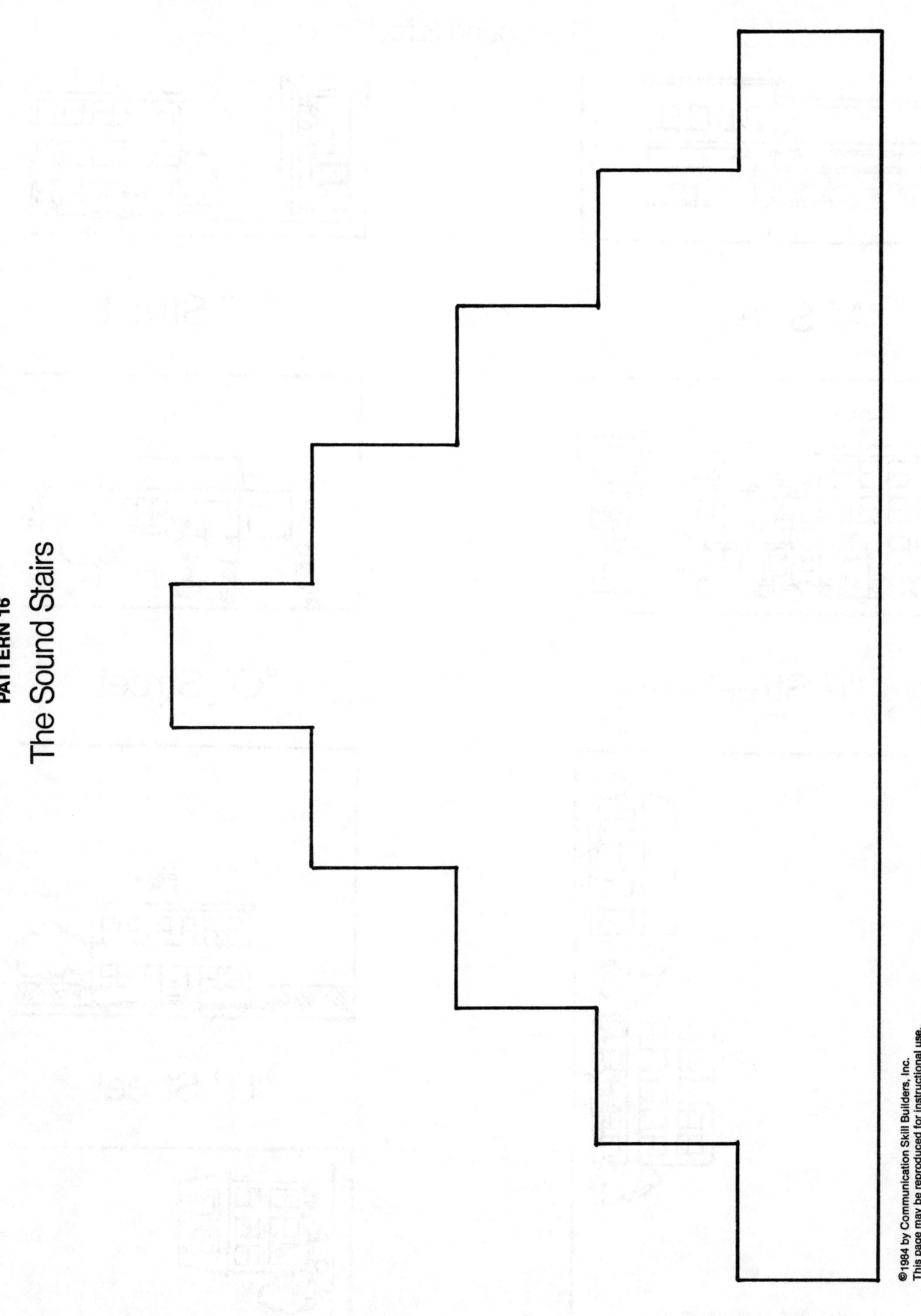

PATTERN 17

The Sound Street

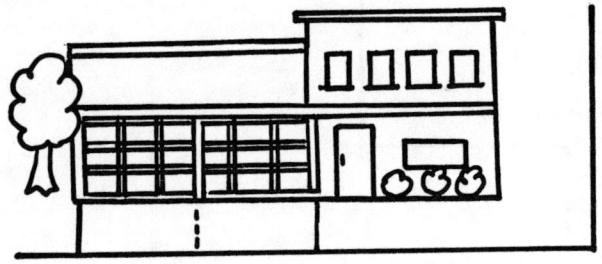

"A" Street

"E" Street

"I" Street

"O" Street

"U" Street

PATTERN 18

The Sound Parachute

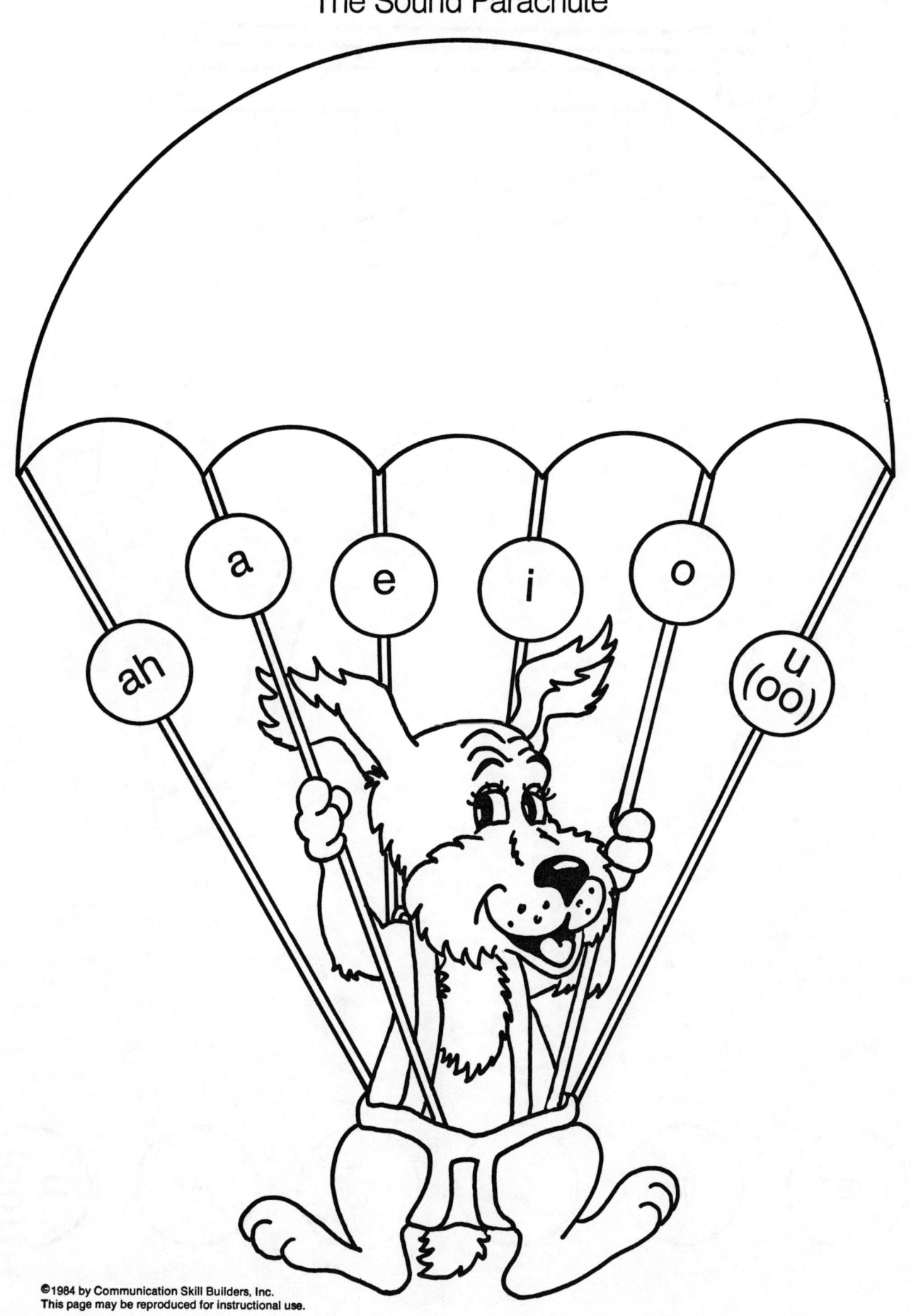

PATTERN 19
The Sound Slide

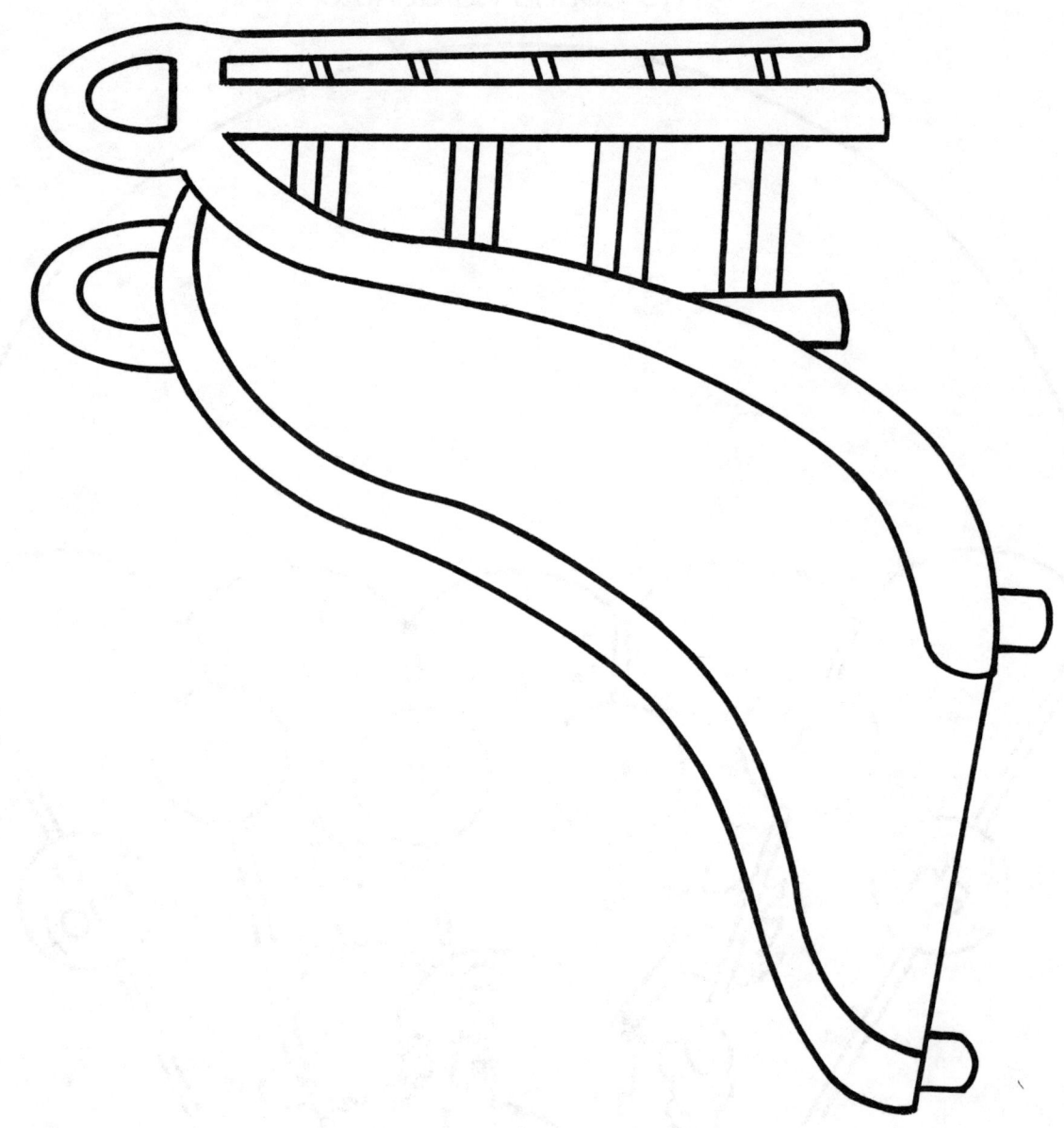

Hide and Say Games

Suggested grade levels: Kindergarten - 2

Objectives: 1. To develop articulation skills
2. To develop visual memory skills

Materials
Stimulus pictures
File folder
Tokens
Paper clips
Glue

Preparation
On the inside of an open file folder, glue ten or more stimulus pictures containing the target phoneme. (Each student may have a folder, or all students may share one.)

Procedures
1. Each student, in turn, chooses a picture; produces the target phoneme in a word, phrase, or sentence; and then covers the picture with a token. When all the pictures have been covered, the students try to remember the locations of the pictures, uncovering each one and responding as before.
2. With eyes closed, the student drops a paper clip onto the board, then names the picture that the paper clip touches. (The pictures may have various point values.)

Sound Mazes

Suggested grade levels: Kindergarten - 2

Objectives: 1. To develop articulation skills
2. To develop fine motor skills

Materials
- Tagboard
- Stimulus pictures
- Glue
- Clear adhesive plastic
- Crayon
- Tissue or soft cloth

Preparation
Reproduce Worksheets 6 and 7 on tagboard. Glue a stimulus picture at each X. Cover with clear adhesive plastic.

Procedure
The student uses a crayon to trace the path to the Happy Face, stopping at each stimulus picture to produce the target word. (Later, the maze may be wiped with a tissue and reused.)

WORKSHEET 6
Sound Maze

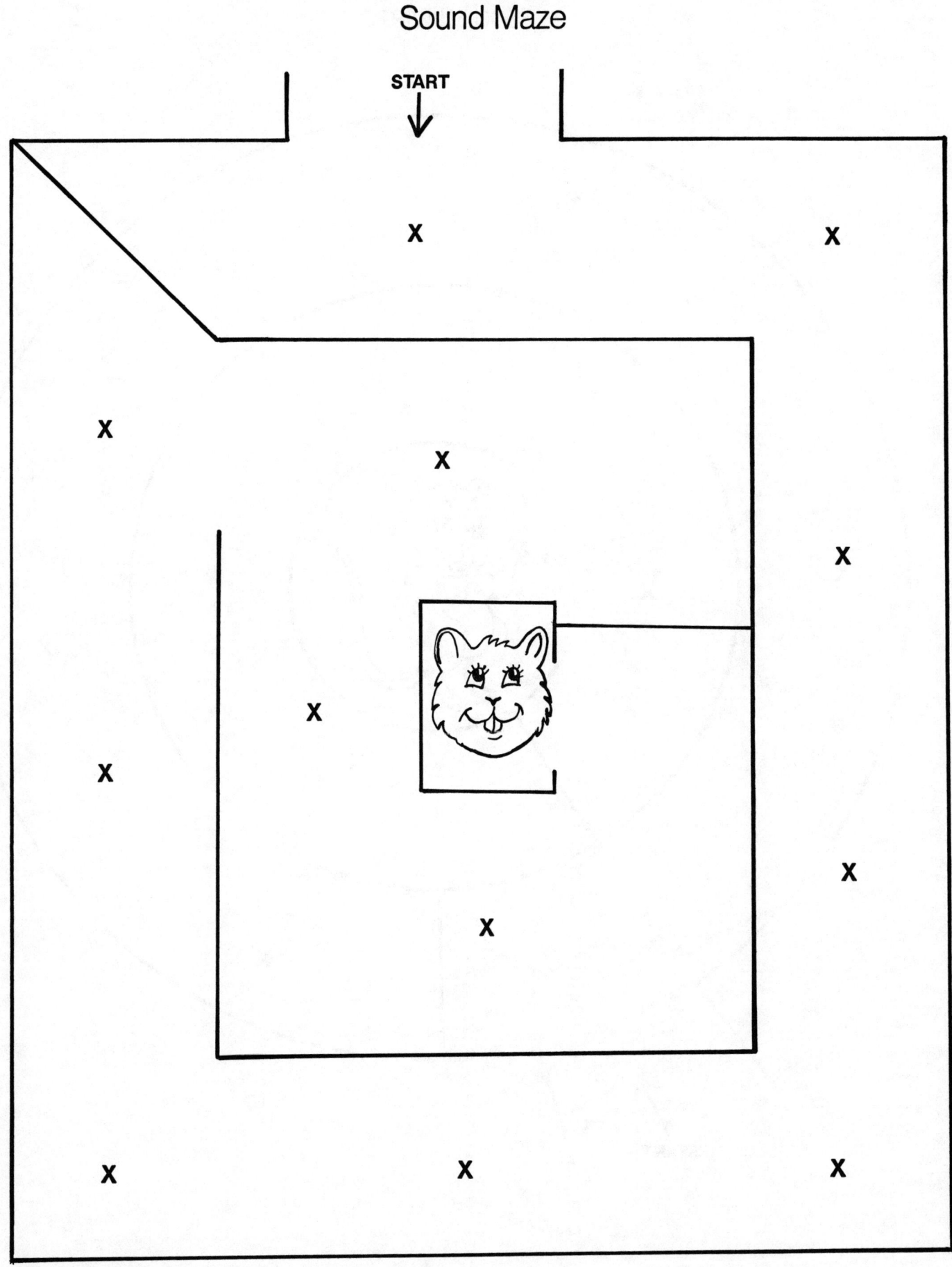

WORKSHEET 7
Sound Maze

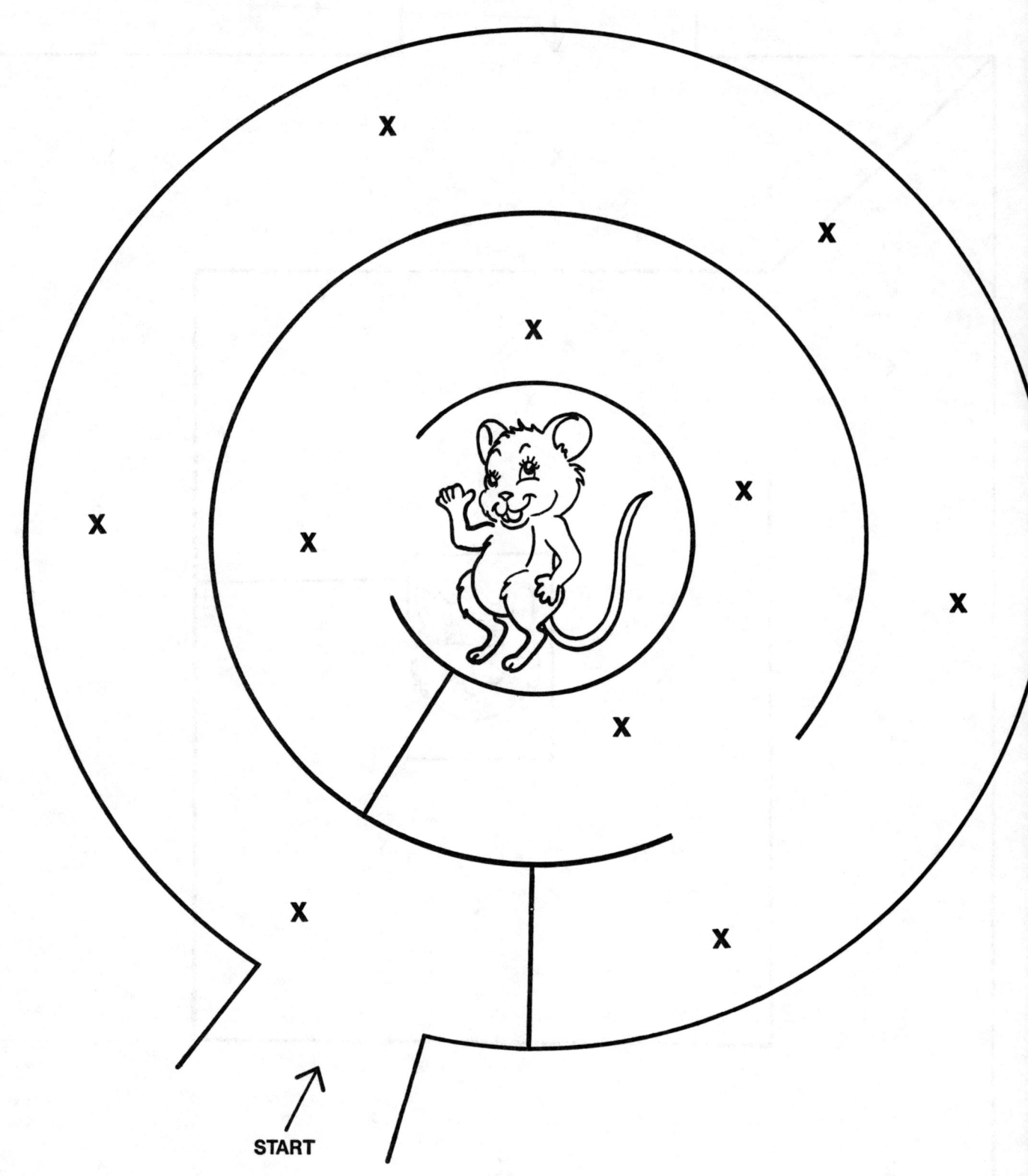

©1984 by Communication Skill Builders, Inc.
This page may be reproduced for instructional use.

Speech Puzzles

Suggested grade levels: Kindergarten - 6

Objectives:
1. To develop articulation skills
2. To develop fine motor skills
3. To develop visual discrimination skills

Materials
- Pictures
- Tagboard
- Glue
- Clear adhesive plastic
- Stimulus cards

Preparation
Select a picture that contains several of the target phoneme sounds. Glue to tagboard. Cover with plastic. Cut into puzzle pieces. Number the back of each piece, and number the stimulus cards the same.

Procedure
Present a stimulus card to the student. After correctly articulating the word, the student is given the puzzle piece that corresponds to the number on the card. When the puzzle is completed, ask the student to describe the picture or tell a story about it.

Two or More

Suggested grade levels: 1 - 6

Objective: To develop articulation skills

Materials
Stimulus cards
Copies of Worksheet 8
Tokens

Preparation
Reproduce Worksheet 8 for each student.

Procedure
Each student selects a stimulus card and produces a phrase or sentence containing the target phoneme. The student moves a token to the next space corresponding to the number of target phonemes in the sentence. For example, if the sentence contained two /r/'s, the token is moved to the next "2" space. The first student to cross the finish line wins the game.

WORKSHEET 8

Two or More

2	3	3	4
1	4	2	5
5	5	1	1
4	1	5	2
3	2	4	3
2	3	3	4
1	4	2	5
5	5	1	1
4	1	5	2
3	2	4	3
2	3	3	4
1	4	2	5
Start	5	1	**Finish**

Word Bingo

Suggested grade levels: 1-6

Objective: To develop articulation skills

Materials
 25 pieces of paper
 Copies of Worksheet 9
 A container

Preparation
Reproduce Worksheet 9 for each student. Write a word containing the target phoneme in each square. Write the same words on each of the 25 pieces of paper. Place the pieces of paper in the container.

Procedure
The student draws one word at a time from the container. After correctly articulating the sounds in the word, the student places the paper on the corresponding square. The student wins when five words in a row are covered (horizontally, vertically, or diagonally).

WORKSHEET 9
Word Bingo

Language Skills

Shapes and Colors

Suggested grade levels: Preschool - 2

Objectives: 1. To develop shape concepts
               2. To develop color concepts

Materials
    Construction paper
    Scissors
    Paper bag

SHAPES

Preparation
    Cut out large shapes (square, rectangle, triangle, circle, or other shapes you wish to teach) from one color of construction paper. Place them on the floor. Cut out four small shapes of each of the large shapes. Place them in the paper bag.

Procedures
1. Each student stands on a different shape. The "caller" (the clinician or a student) takes a shape from the bag and says, "Who's on the _____?" The student standing on that shape responds, "I'm on the _____" and takes the small shape. The first student to get four shapes is the next caller.
2. Each student takes a small shape from the bag, names it, and stands on the corresponding large shape. The procedure continues, with the students moving from shape to shape, until the bag is empty.

COLORS

Preparation
    Cut out four small squares of each of four colors. Place them in the paper bag. Place matching sheets of construction paper on the floor.

Procedures
1. Each student stands on a different color. The "caller" takes a small square from the bag and says, "Who's on _____?" The student standing on that color responds, "I'm on _____" and takes the small square. The first student to get four squares is the next caller.
2. Each student takes a small square from the bag, names the color, and stands on the corresponding colored paper. The procedure continues, with the students moving from color to color, until the bag is empty.

Classification Folders

Suggested grade levels: Preschool - 2

Objective: To develop classification skills

Materials
>File folders
>Stimulus pictures

Preparation
>Divide the pictures into categories (foods, clothing, furniture, transportation, etc.). Place pictures for each category into a separate folder. Decorate the cover of each folder to illustrate the category (a house for the furniture, a grocery store for the food, dresser drawers for clothing).

Procedure
>Mix up the pictures from two or more categories and place them on the table. Describe a situation such as the following: "Susie's mother asked her to clean up her room and put all the toys away. Help Susie put all the furniture in the doll house, all the clothing in the closet, and all the vehicles in the toy garage." The student places the pictures in the appropriate folders.

Holiday Matching

Suggested grade levels: Preschool - 2

Objectives:
1. To develop classification skills
2. To develop color, shape, and size concepts
3. To develop visual discrimination skills

Materials
Construction paper

Preparation
Cut out ten construction paper shapes representing a holiday (eggs for Easter, pumpkins for Halloween, snowflakes for Christmas). Cut the shapes in half. On each half draw a shape (triangle, square, circle, rectangle). Vary the sizes of the shapes and the colors.

Procedure
The student matches up two halves of the holiday shape. Matching may be done by size, color, or shape. The student also may make groupings by size, color, and shape.

Concept File Folder

Suggested grade levels: Kindergarten - 3

Objectives:
1. To develop language concepts
2. To develop classification skills
3. To develop expressive language skills
4. To develop auditory discrimination skills

Materials
File folder
Velcro strips
Stimulus cards
Glue

Preparation
Glue a one-inch strip of Velcro on the back of each stimulus card. Open the file folder and glue two strips of Velcro down the length of the folder.

Procedures
1. *Concepts and Classification*
   The student places all the pictures that represent a concept or category on one side of the folder, and pictures representing a contrasting concept on the other side (for example, big/little, same/different, colors, furniture, vehicles, foods).

2. *Language Structures*
   The student selects a picture for each of two structures (for example, subject/verb), places the pictures on the Velcro strips, and produces an appropriate utterance.

3. *Auditory Discrimination*
   The clinician says each stimulus card. The student places pictures of objects that contain the target phoneme on one side of the folder, and pictures of objects that do not contain the target phoneme on the other side.

Sentence Spin

Suggested grade levels: Kindergarten - 3

Objective: To develop expressive language skills

Materials
- Three 8-inch squares of tagboard
- Pictures of a man, woman, girl, and boy
- Pictures demonstrating actions
- Pictures of objects
- Glue
- Three paper clips
- Three brass fasteners

Preparation
Glue four pictures on each 8-inch square of tagboard. One board should have the pictures of the man, woman, girl, and boy; one board should have the action pictures; and one board should have the object pictures. Construct a spinner on each 8-inch square of tagboard, using the paper clips and brass fasteners.

Procedure
The student will spin the spinners and make a phrase/sentence with the combined pictures.

Clinical Note
If the student is just beginning to combine words, use only two spinners.

Fishbowl

Suggested grade levels: Kindergarten - 3

Objectives: 1. To develop expressive language skills
2. To develop receptive language skills

Materials
Tagboard

Scissors

Crayons or marking pens

A barrier

Preparation
Using Pattern 20, cut out and glue two identical fishbowls on two separate sheets of tagboard. Using Pattern 21, cut out fish, and color them in identical sets of two. Erect a barrier so that two players cannot see each other's fishbowl.

Procedure
Give each player a fishbowl and identical sets of fish. The message-sender places the fish in various locations in, on, and around the fishbowl.

The sender tells the message-receiver which fish to choose and where to place them (for example, "Put a big yellow fish at the top of the tank," or "Put a little blue fish between the yellow fish and the green fish"). The message-receiver may ask the sender questions. At the end of the game, both fishbowls should match. If they do not, the sender should simplify the messages.

Some suggested spatial concepts are:

above/below	next to
over/under	inside/outside
middle	top/bottom
between	right/left

Begin with a few spatial concepts and colors, and gradually increase the complexity of the directions.

PATTERN 20
Fishbowl

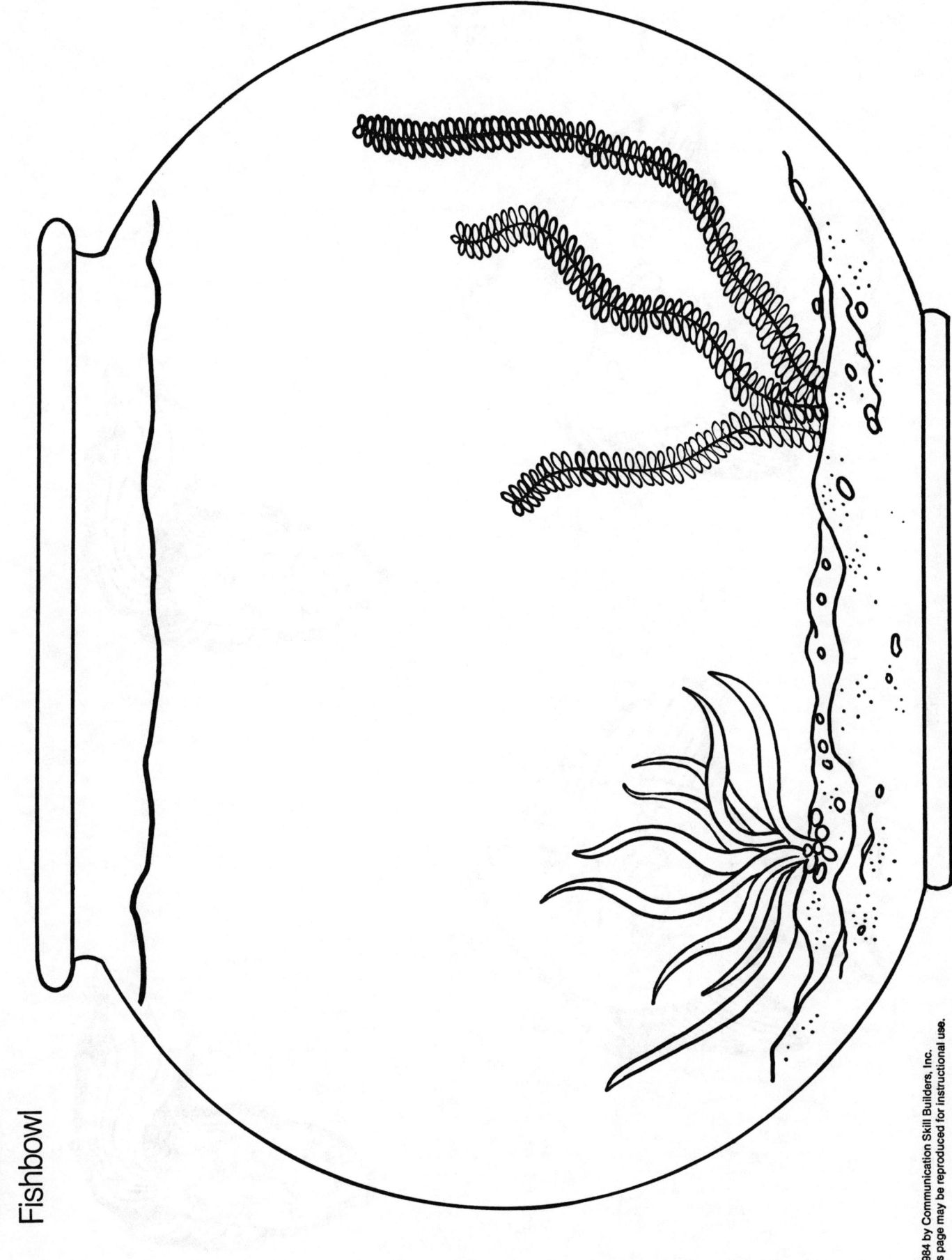

PATTERN 21

Fish

©1984 by Communication Skill Builders, Inc.
This page may be reproduced for instructional use.

Clue Box

Suggested grade levels: Kindergarten - 4

Objectives: 1. To develop reasoning skills
2. To develop classification skills

Materials
  A sturdy box
  Gift wrap
  Yarn

Preparation
  Cover the box with gift wrap so that the box may be opened without unwrapping it. Place an object inside the box, then tie it with yarn. Write several clues to the identity of the object, such as its color, shape, use, texture, beginning sound.

Procedure
  The students are told one clue each day until someone guesses the contents of the box. That student then takes the box home, puts an object in it, and makes up several clues. The box is returned, and the procedure is repeated. Or, one group may choose an object and provide clues to another group.

Language Stimulation Using the Sense of Touch

Suggested grade levels: Kindergarten - 5

Objectives:
1. To develop tactile skills
2. To develop association of pictures and objects
3. To develop expressive language skills

1. WHAT'S IN MY SOCK?

Materials
   10 socks
   10 quart-sized plastic containers
   10 objects (toothbrush, comb, pencil, toy car, etc.)
   A picture of each object

Preparation
   Place an object in each container, then place a container in each sock.

Procedure
   The student reaches into a sock and feels the item inside, describes and names it, finds the matching picture, and places it on top of the container. The procedure is repeated for each sock.

2. TACTILE PICTURES

Materials
   Construction paper
   Scissors
   Glue
   Stimulus pictures
   Textured materials

Some suggested stimulus pictures and textured materials
   A window with panes of plastic food wrap
   A queen with sequins in her crown
   A lamb with cotton or lamb's wool
   A piggy bank with a penny
   A table with a fabric tablecloth
   A rabbit with a cotton-ball tail
   A girl with ribbons in her hair
   A boy with fabric pants (corduroy or denim)
   A room with real carpet

A dog with fake fur material

A kitten with whiskers from broom straw

A window with curtains

Preparation

Make a set of stimulus pictures from coloring books or magazines.

Glue textured materials and the pictures on construction paper.

Procedure

As each picture is presented, the student looks at it, touches the fabric, and describes it.

People-Sorting

Suggested grade levels: Kindergarten - 6

Objectives:
1. To develop expressive language skills
2. To develop classification skills
3. To develop emotion concepts
4. To develop interactive language skills

Materials

Tagboard

Scissors

Glue

Stimulus pictures from magazines, showing activities that elicit different emotions (for example, children at a party, a child getting a gift, a child tracking mud into the house, a parent coming home from work)

Preparation

Cut out the pictures and mount them on tagboard.

Procedure

The student sorts the pictures in some way, and these categories are discussed. The student is encouraged to develop alternative categories.

Then the student role-plays the situation in each picture.

Plurals File Folder

Suggested grade levels: Kindergarten - 6

Objective: To develop the use of plural forms

Materials
    File folder
    Stimulus pictures (two of each item)

Preparation
    Cut one side of a file folder in half (perpendicular to and up to the fold). Put a pair of matching pictures inside the folder, one behind each flap.

Procedure
    The student opens one flap and produces a sentence, using the singular form of the item in the picture. The student then opens the other flap, showing the two pictures. The student produces a sentence, using the plural form. After a correct response, the pictures are removed and another pair is inserted in the folder.

Clinical Note
    Regular plural forms are developed first, followed by irregular forms.

The WH? House

Suggested grade levels: Kindergarten - 3

Objectives:
1. To develop expressive language skills
2. To develop receptive language skills
3. To develop auditory attending skills

Materials
Tagboard
Pictures of household items
Pictures of people doing household tasks
Glue
Envelopes

Preparation
Draw a simple house on a large piece of tagboard. In each room draw items which will help identify that room (for example, bathroom: toilet and tub). In each room, leave a large blank space and attach an envelope.

Procedures
1. Show a picture and ask the student WH questions that require the student to describe the picture. Then tell the student to put the picture in the room where it belongs (put it in the envelope).
2. Ask the student to pretend to be doing a household task or using a household item. Ask the student to identify the appropriate room where the activity is occurring.
3. Describe a pictured item by size, shape, color, use, etc., and have the student guess what it is. If the guess is correct, the student places the picture in the appropriate envelope.

The WH? Spinner

Suggested grade levels: Kindergarten - 8

Objective: To develop expressive language skills

Materials
Tagboard
Brass fastener
Stimulus cards

Preparation
Using Pattern 22, construct a WH spinner from the tagboard and paper fastener.

Procedures
1. The clinician reads a story to the student. The student spins the WH spinner and answers the corresponding WH question, or must formulate a WH question for another student to answer.
2. The clinician selects a picture card and conceals it from the students. Each student spins and asks a WH question about the item (for example, "Who uses it?"). The student who guesses the item selects the next picture card.

PATTERN 22

The WH? Spinner

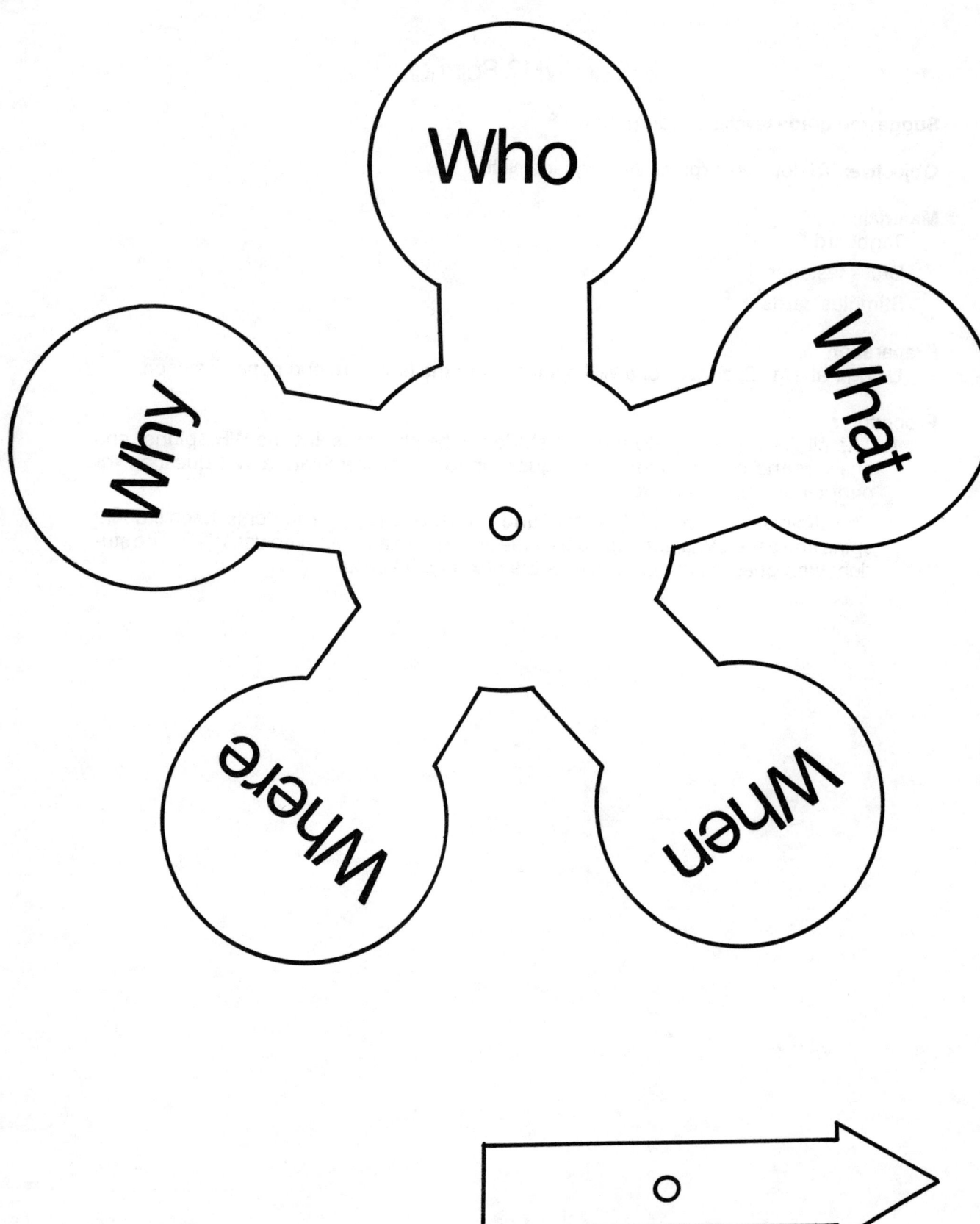

©1984 by Communication Skill Builders, Inc.
This page may be reproduced for instructional use.

Question Games

Suggested grade levels: 2 - 6

Objective: To develop expressive language skills

Materials
    5" x 7" index cards
    Marking pen

Preparation
    Print a series of words or phrases on the cards. Examples could be:
        at night
        kick it
        fingerprints
        around your waist
        ball

Procedures
1. The student draws a card and must make a question relevant so that the card selected will be the answer. Make a list of question words to use as a starter, if necessary (who, what, when, where, how).
2. The student draws two cards at random from the stack. The student must make a sentence using the words on the two cards. (Require a specified number of sentences within a specific time period.)

Treasure Hunt Maze

Suggested grade levels: 3 - 6

Objectives:
1. To develop expressive language skills
2. To develop the ability to follow directions
3. To develop carryover of speech and language skills
4. To develop gross motor skills

Materials
Strips of construction paper or colored tape
Index cards
Red tagboard

Preparation
Place paper strips or tape on the floor around the room in the form of a maze. Make several stop signs from tagboard, and place them at various points along the maze. On index cards, make a direction card and a reward card to place at each stop sign. Examples are:

Direction card: "In a complete sentence tell how you feel."

Reward card: "That was a good sentence. Walk three steps."

Directions should be based on the level of the student and on the therapy objectives. A toy or other reward should be placed at the end of the maze.

Procedure
The student walks through the maze. At each stop, the student reads the direction and responds. If the response is correct, the student reads the reward card and continues on.

Clinical Note
If facilities permit, the maze may extend outside the therapy room to promote carryover of new skills.

Coaster Card Game

Suggested grade levels: 4 - 6

Objective: To develop expressive language skills

Materials
 20 party coasters, or construction paper cut into the shape of coasters

Preparation
 On one side of the coasters, print various speech and language tasks, as listed below.

 Assign each task a numerical value (1 point, 3 points, and 10 points) according to the difficulty of the task.

Procedure
 Spread the coasters face down on the table. Have the student choose one and do the task. Record the score. Repeat four more times. Add the points. Have the student try to beat the previous score by returning the coasters to the pile and beginning again.

COASTER TASKS

1. Say the ABCs.
2. Count from 1 to 10 backwards.
3. Tell me your name, address, and age.
4. What do you want for your birthday present?
5. Who is your favorite rock star? Why?
6. What is your favorite movie? Why?
7. What is your favorite TV show? Why?
8. Tell about a cartoon you saw recently.
9. What did you have for breakfast?
10. Who is your best friend? Why?
11. Who is not your friend? Why?
12. What is your favorite sport? Why?
13. Spell the name of a month.
14. Spell the name of a day of the week.
15. Name three methods of transportation.
16. Name five animals.
17. Name five vegetables.
18. Who is your favorite president? Why?
19. Name five things that are your favorite color.
20. Name two things that weigh the same.
21. Name five things that come in pairs.
22. Name five things that make noise.
23. Name five games that you like to play.
24. What is your favorite school subject? Why?
25. Free choice.

Combination Skills

Seven Easy Puppets

Suggested grade levels: Preschool - 6

Objectives:
1. To develop interactive language skills
2. To develop role-play and imaginative play skills
3. To develop receptive language skills
4. To develop articulation skills
5. To develop expressive language skills

Materials
- Construction paper
- Paper lunch bags
- Scissors
- Crayons or marking pens
- Glue
- ½-pint milk cartons
- Yarn
- Plastic foam cups
- Hamburger cartons (from fast-food restaurants)
- Socks
- Felt, buttons, fabric scraps
- Tongue depressor

1. PAPER BAG PUPPET

Preparation
Reproduce Patterns 23 through 26 on construction paper. Cut out the facial shapes. Hold a folded paper lunch bag upside down, and glue the facial parts to the flap of the bag. Cut out and decorate a body from construction paper. Glue it to the remaining length of the bag. To operate the puppet, insert your hand into the bag with fingers bent to fit into the flap to make the puppet "talk."

2. MILK CARTON PUPPET

Preparation
Cut horizontally through the center of an empty ½-pint milk carton, cutting three sides (the uncut side becomes a hinge). Cut hair, eyes, nose, mouth, and ears from construction paper; glue to the open side of the carton. To operate the puppet, place four fingers on the top section and the thumb on the lower section. Opening and closing the hand makes the puppet "talk."

3. HAMBURGER CARTON PUPPET

Preparation

Make hair, eyes, nose, mouth, and ears from construction paper; glue to the open side of the carton. Cut one hole above the hinge and one hole below the hinge. To operate the puppet, place thumb in the lower hole and two fingers in the upper hole. Opening and closing the hand makes the puppet "talk."

4. PLASTIC-FOAM CUP PUPPET

Preparation

Draw eyes, mouth, and ears on a plastic-foam cup; glue yarn hair. In the space for the nose, cut a small circle. To operate the puppet, insert a finger through the hole.

5. SOCK PUPPET

Preparation

Cut a slit in the end of a sock, and glue red felt around the slit for a mouth; sew on buttons for eyes; glue on yarn hair; decorate with fabric scraps. To operate the puppet, insert your hand into the sock, with four fingers above the mouth and thumb below the mouth. Opening and closing the hand makes the puppet "talk."

6. FOLDED PUPPET

Preparation

Fold a square piece of construction paper in half diagonally. Draw animal features; fold over two corners for ears. To operate the puppet, hold with thumb inside and four fingers outside (or glue the puppet to a tongue depressor).

7. FINGER PUPPET

Preparation

Reproduce and cut out an animal shape from tagboard, using Patterns 27 through 29. Cut out two small holes for inserting fingers. To operate the puppet, insert one finger through each hole, from back to front. Fingers may represent the puppet's ears, arms, or legs.

Procedures

1. *Articulation*
   Name each character, using the target phoneme. The puppet must produce the target phoneme in words, phrases, sentences, or conversational speech.

2. *Receptive Language*
   As the students participate in constructing the puppets, emphasize concepts of color, shape, size, texture, folding, cutting, and body parts.

3. *Expressive Language*
   Ask the students to tell a story, ask questions, or converse using the puppets; or stage a play using puppets.

PATTERN 23

Paper Bag Puppet—Dog

©1984 by Communication Skill Builders, Inc.
This page may be reproduced for instructional use.

PATTERN 24

Paper Bag Puppet—Lion

©1984 by Communication Skill Builders, Inc.
This page may be reproduced for instructional use.

PATTERN 25

Paper Bag Puppet—Bear

©1984 by Communication Skill Builders, Inc.
This page may be reproduced for instructional use.

PATTERN 26

Paper Bag Puppet—Goat

©1984 by Communication Skill Builders, Inc.
This page may be reproduced for instructional use.

PATTERN 27

Finger Puppet—Cat

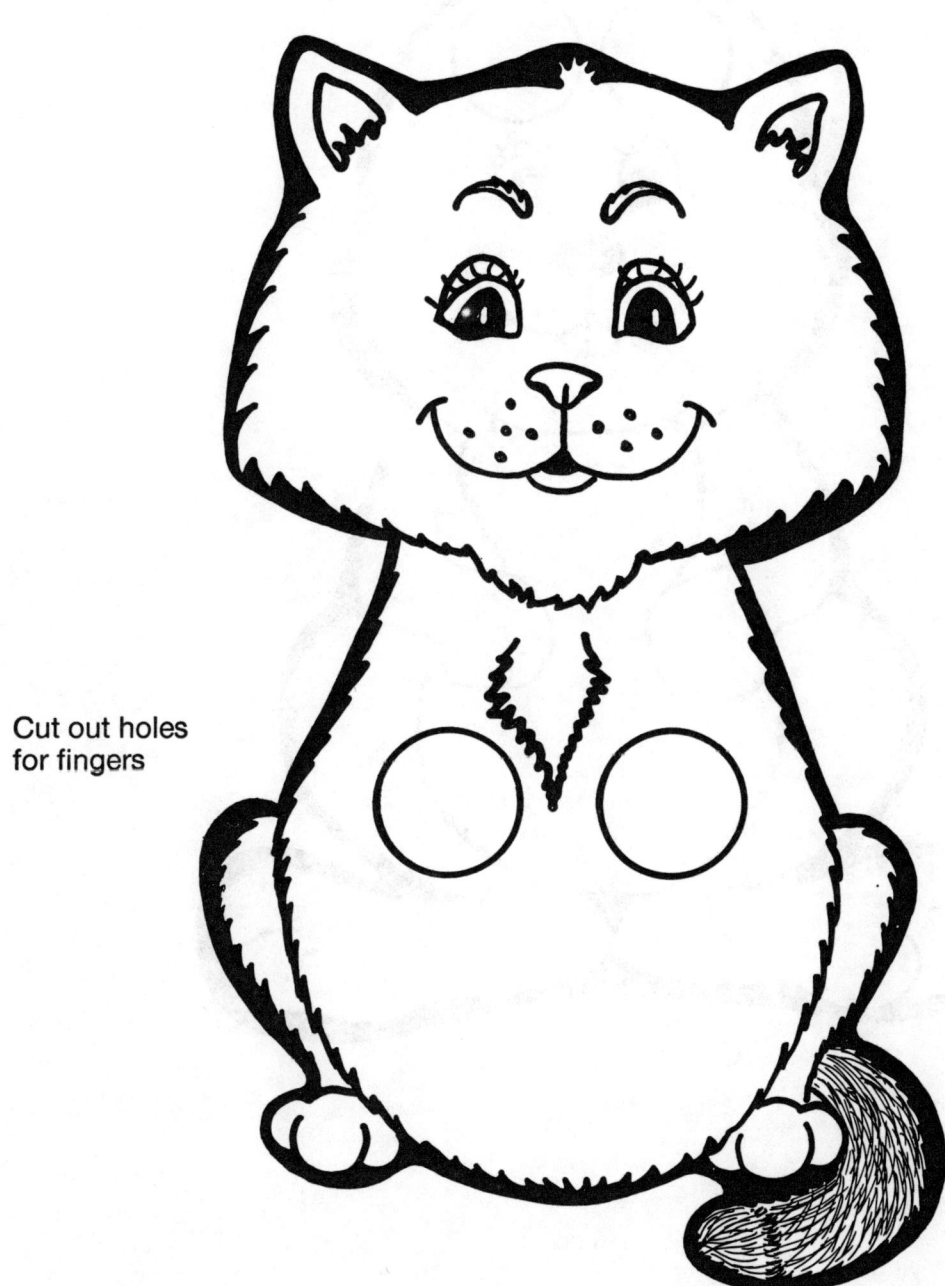

Cut out holes for fingers

©1984 by Communication Skill Builders, Inc.
This page may be reproduced for instructional use.

PATTERN 28

Finger Puppet—Chipmunk

Cut out holes for fingers

©1984 by Communication Skill Builders, Inc.
This page may be reproduced for instructional use.

PATTERN 29

Finger Puppet—Dog

Cut out holes for fingers

©1984 by Communication Skill Builders, Inc.
This page may be reproduced for instructional use.

Battlefield

Suggested grade levels: Preschool - 6

Objectives: 1. To develop articulation skills
                2. To develop expressive language skills

Materials
    File folder
    Paper clips

Preparation
    On the inside of an open file folder, draw lines to make several rows of squares. Label the columns with letters across the top. Label the rows with numbers down one side. Fill in the remaining squares with pictures or written words containing desired target phonemes or language concepts or structures.

Procedure
    Each student secretly chooses a "target" square, either writing it down or telling the clinician. The students take turns trying to guess the other's targets. As each square is chosen, it is covered with a paper clip. Any student who finds a target square gets one point. When choosing a square, the student may be required to produce a sound, word, sentence, or to follow a direction.

Roll the Cubes

Suggested grade levels: Preschool - 6

Objectives:
1. To develop expressive language skills
2. To develop articulation skills
3. To develop auditory discrimination skills

Materials
Cube-shaped pieces of foam rubber
Stimulus cards
Thumbtacks

Preparation
Tack a stimulus card onto each surface of the cube. Make as many cubes as desired.

Procedures
The student rolls the cube and responds according to the stimulus card that faces up.

1. *Language Concepts*
   The student rolls two or more cubes and compares the stimuli according to size, color, shape, sameness, classification, or other relationship.

2. *Language Structures*
   The student rolls two or more cubes, each cube representing a structure such as subject, verb, object, or prepositional phrase. The student produces a complete utterance from the given structures.

3. *Articulation and Auditory Discrimination*
   The student rolls a cube and states whether the stimulus word contains the target phoneme, or states the position of the target phoneme in the word, or produces the word.

Grocery Store

Suggested grade levels: Preschool - 6

Objectives:
1. To develop articulation skills
2. To develop expressive language skills
3. To develop classification skills
4. To develop auditory memory skills
5. To develop interactive language skills

Materials
Empty food containers
Cardboard boxes
Stapler
Tagboard
Marking pens
Grocery sacks

Preparation
Collect empty containers of various grocery items (or have the students contribute containers). Assemble a store area, using shelves built by stacking and stapling together the cardboard boxes. Use tagboard to make a store sign. (Note: If your space is limited, use pictures from advertisements or labels from packages.)

Procedures

1. *Articulation*
Ask the student to purchase items that contain the target phoneme. The student may put the item in the grocery sack after correctly articulating the sound.

2. *Expressive Language*
Role-play grocery shopping. Stimulate production of various syntactical, morphological, and semantic structures.

3. *Classification Skills*
Ask the student to identify items found in the following categories: fruits, vegetables, meat, dairy products, snacks, toiletries, cleaning supplies, paper products; breakfast, lunch, or dinner items; foods that are refrigerated; foods that are cooked.

4. *Auditory Memory*
Name two to seven items. Ask the student to remember and select them from the store.

View-It

Suggested grade levels: Kindergarten - 3

Objective: To develop articulation skills

Materials
    Two toilet tissue tubes
    Ruler
    Spring-type clothespin
    Electrical tape
    Stimulus cards

Preparation
    Tape the tubes together to resemble binoculars. Place them on top of the flat end of a ruler so that the tubes extend 2 inches from beyond the end of the ruler. Secure by winding tape around the tubes and the ruler. At the opposite end of the ruler from the tubes, tape the clothespin with the spring end facing up.

Procedure
    Place a stimulus card in the clothespin. The student looks at the card through the binoculars and responds appropriately.

The Speech Can

Suggested grade levels: Kindergarten - 3

Objectives:
1. To develop articulation skills
2. To develop expressive language skills

Materials
- A coffee can
- Several plastic lids to fit the can
- A ballpoint pen
- Household objects
- Colorful adhesive plastic

ARTICULATION

Preparation

Cover the can with adhesive plastic. Label the lids according to the different sounds being worked on. Fill the can with objects containing the target sound. Cover the can with the appropriately labeled lid.

Procedure

Have the student shake the can with the objects in it, then remove the lid and spill out the contents. Have the student name the objects.

LANGUAGE SKILLS

Preparation

Cover the can with adhesive plastic. Label the lids according to the task (shapes, colors, textures, etc.). Fill the can with appropriate objects (for example, all objects have different textures, distinctive shapes, etc.). Cover the can with the appropriately labeled lid.

Procedure

Use the same procedure as above, but have the student name the objects for vocabulary practice.

Match the Shapes

Suggested grade levels: Kindergarten - 4

Objectives:
1. To develop articulation skills
2. To develop expressive language skills
3. To develop visual discrimination skills
4. To identify shapes

Materials
Tagboard
Construction paper
Stimulus pictures

Preparation
Using Pattern 30, draw all the shapes on one large piece of tagboard. From construction paper, make several sets of stimulus cards to match the shapes on the board.

Procedure
Give each student a set of stimulus cards. After completing the speech or language objective, the student identifies the shape of the card and places it in the matching spot on the board.

PATTERN 30
Shapes

Find the Squirrel

Suggested grade levels: Kindergarten - 4

Objectives: 1. To develop articulation skills
2. To develop expressive language skills

Materials
- A file folder
- Construction paper
- Tagboard
- Scissors
- Glue
- A marking pen
- Four markers
- A die
- Stimulus cards

Preparation
Make four trees from construction paper, using Pattern 31. Make a "forest" by gluing the trees along the edge of the opened file folder. On the folder, designate four starting points and draw footprints leading along four paths to the trees. Make one squirrel, using Pattern 32. Cut the tagboard into four 1-inch by 4-inch strips, and glue the squirrel to the narrow end of one strip.

Procedure
Place a strip behind each tree, hiding the squirrel in a treetop. (The end of each strip should stick out from behind a tree, so the students can grasp them later.) Each player chooses a path into the forest. In turn, the students select a stimulus card and complete a speech or language objective; roll the die; and move their marker along the corresponding number of footprints. When reaching a tree, the student pulls out the strip. The player who finds the squirrel wins the game.

PATTERN 31

Tree

PATTERN 32

Squirrel

©1984 by Communication Skill Builders, Inc.
This page may be reproduced for instructional use.

Articulation/Language Spinner

Suggested grade levels: Kindergarten - 6

Objectives:
1. To develop articulation skills
2. To develop expressive language skills

Materials
Tagboard
Brass fastener
Glue
Stimulus pictures

Preparation
Make a 12-inch circle of tagboard. Divide the circle into eight sections. Glue several stimulus pictures in each section. Make an arrow from the tagboard, and fasten it to the center of the circle to make a spinner.

Procedures
1. The student spins the spinner and names each stimulus picture in that section that has the target phoneme.
2. The student spins the spinner and selects one picture to describe. Encourage the student to describe the object's function, color, shape, and composition.

Magic Number Board

Suggested grade levels: Kindergarten - 6

Objectives:
1. To develop articulation skills
2. To develop expressive language skills

Materials
File folder
Stimulus cards

Preparation
On the inside of an open file folder, draw ten large squares. Number each square from 1 to 10. Write a corresponding number on the back of each stimulus card.

Procedures
1. Give each student a stack of stimulus cards with the numbers face down. One student chooses the "magic" or "winning" number. In turn, each turns over the top card and places it on the appropriate numbered square. The first student to turn up a card with the winning number gets one point.
2. The students take turns placing cards on the board, as above. The student who covers the last remaining blank square gets one point. For each stimulus card played, the student must respond with a sound, syllable, word, or sentence, as directed by the clinician.

Target Word Board

Suggested grade levels: Kindergarten - 6

Objectives: 1. To develop articulation skills
2. To develop expressive language skills

Materials
Tagboard
Stimulus cards

Preparation
On a piece of tagboard of desired size, cut slits for inserting the corners of stimulus cards. One stimulus card is placed in the center of the board, and other cards are placed around the board. The target word is placed in the center of the board. (The target word may be one in which the target phoneme is correctly produced or a language structure which requires practice in a variety of contexts.) The remainder of the spaces on the board are filled in with desired stimulus cards.

Procedures
1. *Articulation Drill*
The student alternately produces the target word, then a surrounding word, then the target word again, then another surrounding word, continuing until all the surrounding words have been produced.

2. *Language Drill*
The target word is combined with each of the surrounding words in turn, to make complete utterances.

Clinical Note
Classification activities may be done with two or more of these boards, with the student placing each picture on the appropriate board.

Circle Drill

Suggested grade levels: Kindergarten - 6

Objectives:
1. To develop articulation skills
2. To develop receptive language skills
3. To develop expressive language skills

Materials
File folder
Construction paper
Brass fastener
Stimulus pictures
Glue

Preparation
Cut a 7-inch circle from construction paper. Draw eight pie-shaped segments on the circle, then put a word or picture in each segment. Place the circle inside a file folder. Fasten it with a brass fastener that is put through both sides of the file folder as well as through the center of the circle. Through one side of the folder, cut a section large enough to see one stimulus word or picture. Several circles may be made and used interchangeably.

ARTICULATION

Procedures
1. The student turns the wheel and names the picture that shows through the window.
2. Construct wheels containing the following word fragments:

_____ ay	_____ oad
_____ ate	_____ oose
_____ ake	_____ ap
_____ aid	_____ ip
_____ eaf	_____ eg
_____ eave	_____ ove
_____ ie	_____ earn
_____ ike	_____ ift
_____ ight	_____ ook
_____ ow	_____ og

The student produces one of the syllables, inserting the target phoneme in the initial position. The student decides whether or not the syllable is a word. If it is, the word is produced in a sentence.

LANGUAGE

Procedure
Construct a wheel containing pictures that depict various spatial relationships. The student turns the wheel and performs the spatial relation depicted. The student then asks someone "Where is _____?" and the other student responds with an utterance.

Toy Town

Suggested grade levels: Kindergarten - 6

Objectives:
1. To develop articulation skills
2. To develop expressive language skills
3. To develop auditory memory skills

Materials
Tagboard
Marking pens
Empty milk cartons (optional)
A bell
Miniature cars or other tokens

Preparation
Make a map of a town on a sheet of tagboard. (Three-dimensional buildings, bridges, and tunnels may be made from empty milk cartons of various sizes, and placed on the map.)

Procedure
The students take a trip through the town, tracing their paths on the map with tokens and describing where they are going. At each stop, they purchase something that contains the target phoneme. The speaker is monitored by the other students. If they hear an incorrect response, they ring the bell. The speaker must correct the error and surrender the town to the student who rang the bell. At the end of the session, each student reviews the path taken and the purchases made.

TV Talk

Suggested grade levels: Kindergarten - 6

Objectives:
1. To develop articulation skills
2. To develop expressive language skills

Materials
- File folder
- Ruler
- Marking pens
- Acetate page protector
- Scissors
- Glue
- Pictures (full page size)

Preparation

Cut out a square from the front of the file folder. Leave a 2-inch margin on all sides.

In the bottom margin (the open end), draw three circles and color them. Mark one the on-off knob, the other the channel selector, and the last one the color adjustment.

Glue or tape the page protector to the inside of the cut-out side, to make the TV screen.

Procedures
1. Have the student select pictures from magazines, insert a picture, and describe it.
2. The student selects a picture and decides if it's an advertisement, news item, scene from a show, or sports event. The student then acts as the salesperson, newscaster, actor, or sports announcer, making up an original script or reading from the accompanying item in the magazine.
3. The student displays a good speech paper, reinforcement, or school paper for the family to see. Later, the student tells the family about the good paper, to promote carry-over of speech and language skills.

Concentration

Suggested grade levels: Kindergarten - 6

Objectives: 1. To develop articulation skills
2. To develop receptive language skills
3. To develop expressive language skills
4. To develop visual memory skills

Materials
Stimulus cards

Preparation
Assemble sets of stimulus cards matched in the following ways:
1. Pairs that contain the target phoneme, such as sun/sun, bus/bus
2. Pairs that contain the target phoneme in the same position, such as sun/sock, mouse/house
3. Pairs that match categories, such as apple/orange (fruits), car/plane (transportation)
4. Pairs that have an associative response, such as lock/key, shoe/sock

Procedure
Have the students place one set of stimulus cards face down on the table, naming each card as it is placed. Deal the matching set of stimulus cards among the students, who take turns drawing for a match. When a match is made, the student correctly produces the word and describes why it is a match. The student continues to play as long as a match is made each time.

Newspaper Activities

Suggested grade levels: 1 - 6

Objectives: 1. To develop expressive language skills
2. To develop articulation skills
3. To increase carryover of speech and language skills

Materials
Old newspapers
A spiralbound notebook or construction paper stapled into booklet form
Glue

Preparation
Assemble cutouts from newspapers.

Procedures
1. *Sequencing*
   The student arranges the squares of a comic strip in sequential order and glues them on the Funnies page.

2. *Classification*
   a. The student composes an advertisement for a cut-out picture. The description may include size, shape, color, texture, function, price, where the item may be purchased, how and where it was made, why the item is desirable.
   b. The student interviews a person and reports on physical characteristics, activities, job, and hobbies.

3. *Sentence Structures*
   The student describes a sports activity and illustrates it with a drawing or newspaper photo. Emphasis is placed on actions, spatial relationships, and equipment used in the sport.

4. *Combination skills*
   The student composes a current events article with an appropriate headline and illustrates it with a newspaper photo. Speech/language requirements are set by the clinician.

5. *Community helpers*
   The student composes employment ads, describing a job and the qualifications and skills required.

Clinical Note
The articles may be dictated to the clinician, or the student may write the assignments. The student is encouraged to take the "newspaper" home for additional reinforcement.

Role-Playing Activities

Suggested grade levels: Kindergarten - 3 and 4 - 6

Objectives:
1. To develop articulation skills
2. To develop expressive language skills
3. To develop interactive language skills

Materials
- Tagboard
- Tape
- Glue
- Sequins
- Old jewelry
- Aluminum foil
- Newspaper
- Scraps of fabric

Preparation
Make several hats out of tagboard, as explained on pages 120-122.

Procedures
1. *Role-playing* (Kindergarten - 3)
   The clinician discusses hats as a means of identifying what a person does. The student is allowed to select a hat and then tells what the person does and what the person might say. The student then is asked to role-play (see Worksheet 10), monitoring productions as directed by the clinician.

2. *Role-playing* (Grades 4 - 6)
   The student is directed to role-play (see Worksheet 11), monitoring productions as directed by the clinician.

SOLDIER, SAILOR, OR ROBIN HOOD HAT

Directions: Fold 12" x 18" construction paper or a newspaper in half. With folded edge at the top, bring the two upper corners to meet at the center. Fold bottom flaps up on both sides and secure with tape.

NURSE'S HAT

Directions: Fold one side of 8½" x 11" paper back approximately 1½". Bring corners of unfolded edge together and overlap approximately 1". Secure with tape.

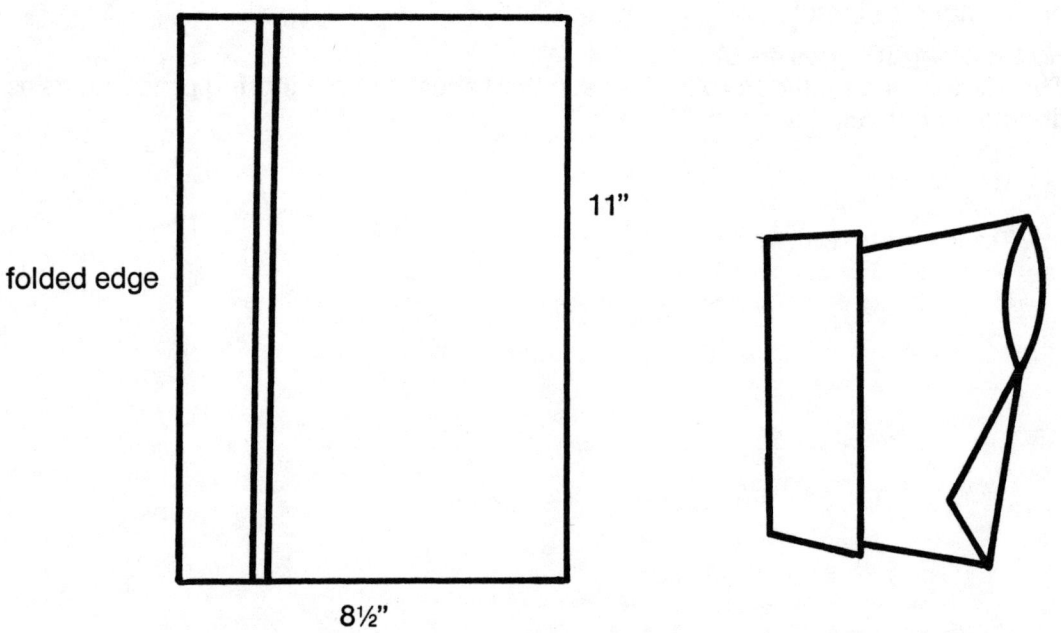

MAGICIAN, PILGRIM, OR RINGMASTER'S HAT

Directions: Use construction paper to make a tall paper tube that fits the head. Cut a circle to fit the top. Cut a ring for the brim. Tape top and brim to tube. Decorate, if desired.

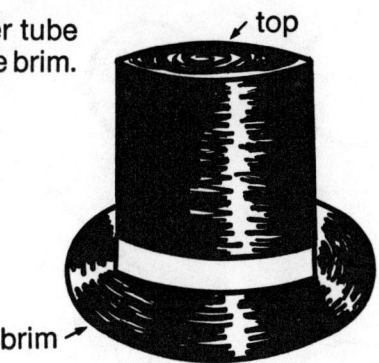

CLOWN OR WITCH'S HAT

Directions: Use construction paper or tagboard to form a cone shape that fits the head. For a clown's hat, add yarn at the top. Decorate as desired.

QUEEN, KING, OR PRINCESS CROWN

Directions: Trace Pattern 33 on construction paper or tagboard. Increase length to 18" or size of child's head. Cover with foil or decorate with sequins.

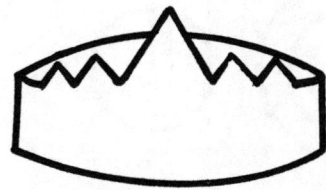

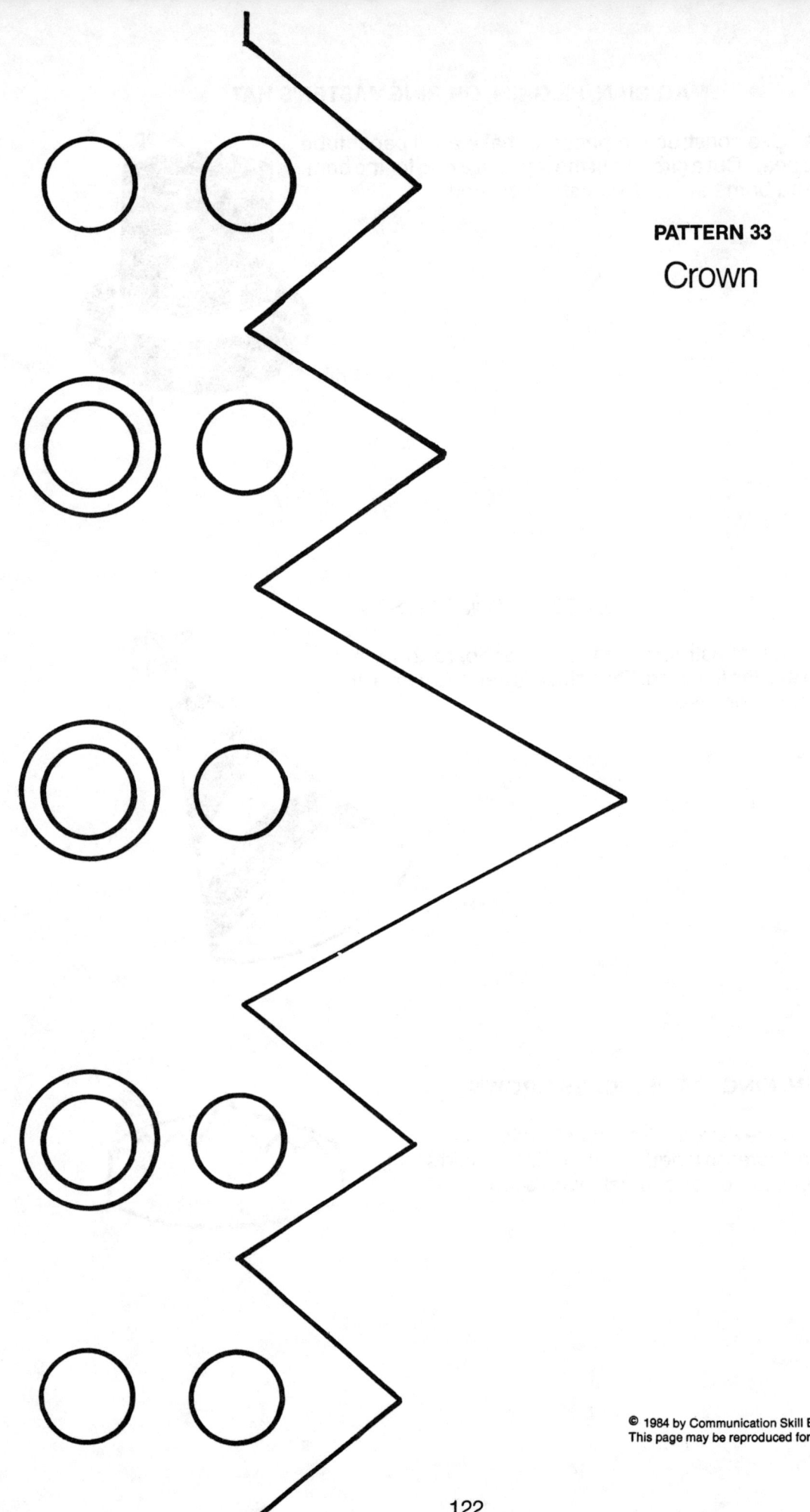

PATTERN 33
Crown

WORKSHEET 10

Role-Playing Activities (Kindergarten - 3)

1. Pretend to be Robin Hood in the forest with his men.
2. Pretend to be a sailor on a big ship.
3. Pretend to be a soldier coming home.
4. Pretend to be a nurse taking care of someone sick.
5. Pretend to be a good queen telling her princesses what to do.
6. Pretend to be a magician at a magic show.
7. Pretend to be the "wicked witch of the North."
8. Pretend to be a circus clown doing tricks.
9. Pretend to be a fire fighter putting out a fire.
10. Pretend to be a police officer helping children to cross the street.

WORKSHEET 11

Role-Playing Activities (Grades 4 - 6)

1. You forgot your lunch for the third time this week. Convince your mother to bring it to school.

2. You want a pet. Convince your parents you will be responsible for it.

3. There's a special program on TV after your bedtime. Persuade your parents to let you stay up.

4. You feel you're too old for a babysitter after school. Explain why you should be allowed to stay home alone.

5. You want to have a slumber party. Ask your parents.

6. Everyone on the block has a skateboard, but your mom thinks they're dangerous. Explain why you need one.

7. You're a witness to an automobile accident. Give your report to the police.

8. You must sell fifty boxes of candy by the end of the week to earn money for a school trip. Sell some.

9. You got an "A" in the class but a "poor" in citizenship. Convince your parents this is undeserved.

10. You've just been shortchanged at the bank. Get your money!

11. Convince your mother or father to stop smoking.

12. Your teacher just called on you for your book report. Explain why you don't have it.

13. Someone at school has started a nasty rumor about you. Approach this person.

14. You run into your mother at the mall when you should be at school. Explain why you're there.

15. You would like to become a newspaper carrier. You are at your interview now.

Santa's Speech

Suggested grade levels: Kindergarten - 6

Objectives: 1. To develop articulation skills
2. To develop expressive language skills

Materials
  Tagboard
  Construction paper
  Stimulus pictures
  Glue
  Scissors

Preparation
Make Santa from construction paper, using Pattern 34. Cut out Santa's mouth. Cut the tagboard into 1-inch by 12-inch strips. Paste stimulus pictures at 1½-inch intervals on the strips.

Preparation
  1. *Articulation*
  The student places a tagboard strip behind Santa's mouth, selects a stimulus picture, produces the stimulus word in a phrase or sentence, and then slides the strip to the next picture.

  2. *Language*
  The student places a tagboard strip behind Santa's mouth, selects a stimulus picture, describes the picture for other students to guess, and then slides the strip to the next picture.

PATTERN 34

Santa's Speech

©1984 by Communication Skill Builders, Inc.
This page may be reproduced for instructional use.

More reproducibles for language from Communication Skill Builders...

TALK IT UP: 40 Games for Language Reinforcement and Remediation (1984)
by Dianne Schoenfeld Barad

> Here's a handy folder of high-interest activities to boost language skills. You can expand your students' verbal expression and save your planning time with these photocopiable gamesheets. These ready-to-use activities focus on classification, association, and using descriptive language. **Catalog No. 7021-Y** **$15.95**

SPEEECH, LANGUAGE, AND READING WORKSHEETS: Fun with Language (1983)
by Margaret F. Smith

> Complete your total speech program with these 81 copiable pages. Here are effective and economical worksheet activities to help you integrate your therapy program with your students' classroom work—valuable for home carryover, too. Each page presents a task clearly with simple line drawings. The 3-ring binder offers easy organization.
> **Catalog No. 4636-Y** **$21.95**

WORDS AND SOUNDS AHOY! (1983) *by Dianne Schoenfeld Barad*

> A cornucopia of language and articulation games! These reproducible "bingo" sheets provide a multitude of activities. You can offer versatile language games for classification, association, vocabulary, and more. You'll also present enjoyable articulation activities for 11 target sounds. You can also use this familiar game format for effective home carryover.
> **Catalog No. 4692-Y** **$15.95**

EASY AS 1-2-3 (1982) *by Constance F. McCarthy and Ann D. Sheehy*

> Reproduce these three-step sequences to reinforce language-learning skills. Each of these 20 quick-to-copy sheets shows three clear line illustrations of a child engaged in a specific activity. Your students put the pictures in order so the sequence makes sense. Directions are easy to follow and include specific objectives for coloring, cutting, sequencing, pasting, and oral expression. **Catalog No. 4612-Y** **$12.95**

PICTURES, PLEASE! An Articulation Supplement (1983)
PICTURES, PLEASE! A Language Supplement (1979)
by Marcia Stevenson Abbate and Nancy Bartell LaChappelle

> Two volumes of reproducible clear line illustrations hold more than 2,000 pictures. You can photocopy each page of drawings over and over again for an unlimited variety of activities. Both of these binders are tab-indexed and all the pictures are cross-referenced. You can easily find the illustrations you need for language and articulation therapy.
> Pictures, Please! An Articulation Supplement   Catalog No. 2091-Y $39
> Pictures, Please! A Language Supplement   Catalog No. 3092-Y $39

Communication Skill Builders
3130 N. Dodge Blvd./P.O. Box 42050
Tucson, Arizona 85733
(602) 323-7500